Natural Great Perfection

Dzogchen Teachings and Vajra Songs

Natural Great Perfection
Dzogchen Teachings and Vajra Songs

by Nyoshul Khenpo Rinpoche
and Lama Surya Das

Snow Lion Publications
Ithaca, New York USA

Snow Lion Publications
P.O. Box 6483
Ithaca, New York 14851 USA

First Edition USA 1995

ISBN 1-55939-049-2

Library of Congress Cataloging-in-Publication Data
Nyoshul Khenpo, Rinpoche, 1932-
    Natural great perfection : Dzogchen teachings and Vajra songs / by
Nyoshul Khenpo Rinpoche and Lama Surya Das. — 1st ed.
        p. cm.
    ISBN 1-55939-049-2
    1. Rdzogs-chen (Rñiṅ-ma-pa)   I. Das, Surya. II. Title.
BQ7662.4.N96   1995
  294.3'923—dc20   95-15875
                                                                         CIP

Contents

Preface

Nyoshul Khenpo Rinpoche is one of the foremost *khenpos* (abbot-professors) of the most ancient school of Tibetan Buddhism, the Nyingma Order, and an important lineage holder of the Dzogchen teachings. An extraordinary Tibetan lama—one of the few remaining senior masters fully trained in Tibet—he is the teacher of many contemporary lamas, and more recently, of numerous Western Dharma teachers.

Khenpo Rinpoche and his wife, Damchö Zangmo, reside mainly in Bhutan, the sole independent Buddhist country remaining in the Himalayas. From there they travel regularly to teach in India, Nepal, Taiwan, France, Switzerland, and North America. Recently, Khenpo has twice visited his native land of Tibet, where he hopes to build a hospital near Palyul.

Nyoshul Khen Rinpoche is a remarkable meditation master, scholar, poet, and storyteller, and a living exemplar of the Buddha's teachings. He trained at Katok Monastery in Kham, one of the six major Nyingmapa monasteries in Tibet, and has also studied and practiced with many of the greatest lamas of different lineages of the previous generation.

He has written two books chronicling the lives and times of the lineage holders of the Dzogchen Nyingthig tradition, which form the basis of the history of the Dzogchen lineage in this present volume. Two dozen of Khenpo's extemporaneous *vajra*-songs (*dohas*) have been translated by the Padmakara Translation Group in France. A dozen of them appeared in 1988 in an English-language publication from Rigpa Publications entitled *Rest in Natural Great*

Peace: Songs by Nyoshul Khenpo Rinpoche. Rinpoche's vajra-songs were often penned spontaneously with magic markers in large scrawled letters on sheets of paper towels, on paper napkins, or on whatever Khenpo found at hand on the spur of the moment. In most cases they were sung spontaneously for various individuals, and afterwards repeated at the students' request, to be recorded, transcribed, and translated.

Khenpo Rinpoche is also, like many lamas, a repository of the treasure trove of profound Buddhadharma, as well as a funny and fascinating storyteller. Although he has limited vocal capacity, due to chronic illness, he continuously overflows with the oral lore and Buddhist law that inform the wisdom tales of Tibet. At least two dozen of the 150 teaching tales and stories collected in my book, *The Snow Lion's Turquoise Mane: Wisdom Tales from Tibet* (Harper San Francisco, 1992) were told to me by Nyoshul Khenpo.

During the 1980's, Khenpo Rinpoche taught for several years at the Nyingma and Kagyu three-year retreats in the Dordogne Valley in southern France. I first met Nyoshul Khenpo in 1973, at Riwoche Kangyur Rinpoche's monastery in Darjeeling, while he was suffering from the effects of a stroke and being nursed by Kangyur Rinpoche's family. But it was not until eight years later— when my Dharma friends and I actually had the opportunity to live and study closely with him for several years at Dilgo Khyentse Rinpoche's Chanteloube Retreat center in Dordogne—that I began to appreciate what a truly gifted spiritual teacher and yogi he is. Through his personal guidance and instructions he had a profound effect on my meditation practice and understanding during those years in secluded retreat in the forest. I remain forever grateful for his immense kindness in this regard; for it is not a teacher's status, title, renown, or even friendship that is ultimately meaningful to a disciple, but it is the actual impact he or she has on that student's life and development that really matters.

Khenpo Sonam Tobgyal Rinpoche, originally a monk from Riwoche Monastery in Tibet, was Nyoshul Khenpo's attendant and main student during that time in France. When Lama Sonam moved to Canada to teach, and then stayed to establish a Riwoche center in Toronto, I had the good fortune to serve as Khenpo

Rinpoche's personal attendant, and occasionally as his interpreter. It was during that period that he asked me to jot down and record for posterity the oral teaching tales of our lineage.

In 1990 Nyoshul Khen Rinpoche returned to Tibet for the first time since the Red Chinese took control of his homeland in 1959. I was fortunate to be part of that pilgrimage, which was headed by our root guru, H.H. Dilgo Khyentse Rinpoche. Since 1993, Khen Rinpoche has made three annual visits to the United States at my invitation: leading retreats, receiving medical treatment, resting, and occasionally teaching at other Dharma centers in North America.

Dzogchen, the innate Great Perfection, is "the teaching for today," as many masters have said. Just to be in the presence of an authentic Dzogchen master introduces one's own true nature. Nyoshul Khenpo's joyous, radiant presence exudes these vast and profound teachings. This book is a small attempt to share some of the timeless wisdom that Nyoshul Khenpo and other Buddhist masters like him have to offer, in a form accessible and meaningful for today.

I would like to gratefully acknowledge the work of the talented translators who contributed to this volume: Venerable Matthieu Ricard, Erik Schmidt, Ani Lodrö Palmo, Ward Brisick, the Padmakara Translation Group in Dordogne, France, David Christensen, Corinna Chung, and Charles Hastings. I also wish to thank Suzanne Fairclough, Linda Mathiasen, Terry Brennan, and Anasuya Weil for their help in transcribing and preparing this manuscript for publication, and my editor at Snow Lion Publications, David Patt. And special thanks and gratitude to Tulku Pema Wangyal Rinpoche and his family, for everything.

May any merits accrued through this work be dedicated towards the longevity and continuing availability of these spiritual teachers and teachings.

Sarva mangalam. May all be auspicious!

Lama Surya Das
Cambridge, Massachusetts

The ancient "Talking Guru Rinpoche" statue at Samye Chimphu, Tibet. This image of Padmasambhava belonged to Vairotsana, one of the earliest patriarchs of the Dzogchen lineage in Tibet. Photo courtesy of the author.

Prologue
Free and Easy: A Spontaneous Vajra Song

by Venerable Lama Gendun Rinpoche

Happiness cannot be found
through great effort and willpower,
but is already present, in open relaxation and letting go.

Don't strain yourself,
there is nothing to do or undo.
Whatever momentarily arises in the body-mind
has no real importance at all,
has little reality whatsoever.
Why identify with, and become attached to it,
passing judgment upon it and ourselves?

Far better to simply
let the entire game happen on its own,
springing up and falling back like waves—
without changing or manipulating anything—
and notice how everything vanishes and
reappears, magically, again and again,
time without end.

Only our searching for happiness
prevents us from seeing it.
It's like a vivid rainbow which you pursue without ever catching,
or a dog chasing its own tail.

Although peace and happiness do not exist
as an actual thing or place,
it is always available
and accompanies you every instant.

Don't believe in the reality
of good and bad experiences;
they are like today's ephemeral weather,
like rainbows in the sky.

Wanting to grasp the ungraspable,
you exhaust yourself in vain.
As soon as you open and relax this tight fist of grasping,
infinite space is there—open, inviting and comfortable.

Make use of this spaciousness, this freedom and natural ease.
Don't search any further.
Don't go into the tangled jungle
looking for the great awakened elephant,
who is already resting quietly at home
in front of your own hearth.

Nothing to do or undo,
nothing to force,
nothing to want,
and nothing missing—

Emaho! Marvelous!
Everything happens by itself.

*Gendun Rinpoche is a senior Kagyu lama, abbot and retreat master
of Dakpo Kagyu Ling Monastery in Dordogne, France, where this
poem was translated from Tibetan.*

1 Enlightened Vagabond

An Autobiographical Sketch

This is not a *namthar*—a spiritual biography—at all, it's just a series of mishaps. I was born in eastern Tibet in 1932. My father was a roaming bandit, a highwayman. He beat, robbed, and even killed people. I didn't really know my father, because he abandoned his family when I was very young. Father was like the people you see in a cowboy movie, outlaws riding on horses. He habitually lived in the wilderness of Kham, in eastern Tibet.

In my immediate family there were three boys and seven girls. Two of the brothers were very strong and rough, like their father; he strongly favored those two tough boys. I was the third boy, and a bit of a wimp. My father often put me down, saying that I was like a girl and of no use at all. My father taught his children to fight, but the daughters and I didn't like to fight very much, so our father ignored us.

My mother was a very gentle and loving soul, a very dharmic or religious person, with a lot of patience and forbearance. She had sincere aspirations to practice the Dharma, although she had so many children and so much to cope with at home. She harbored great hopes that I would fulfill her aspirations in the Dharma, since I took after her in being gentle and loving. My mother contented herself with the simple rewards of morality, prayer, and devoting herself to her family.

My paternal grandmother, the highwayman's mother, was also pious. She was an occasional disciple of the great Dzogchen master Nyoshul Lungtok Tenpai Nyima, who was Patrul Rinpoche's heart-disciple. Well versed in Dharma and practice, she wasn't very learned but she had received teachings and had practiced and understood them, thus transforming her nature. She prayed constantly that her wayward highwayman son would reform and change his ways.

When I was a baby, my grandmother and my mother would chant again and again over my cradle, "We take refuge in the Buddha, we take refuge in the Dharma, we take refuge in the Sangha." Also, they used to pray and talk to each other about the teachings, and pray to Nyoshul Lungtok Tenpai Nyima, wherever he was—they often didn't even know where he was—fervently expressing their heartfelt wish that he would come to teach and bless them. They reminded each other what a great master he was. That was the first time that I heard this guru's sacred name, Nyoshul Lungtok—a name that inspires me to this day.

When I was older, my grandmother explained to me that Nyoshul Lungtok was her revered root lama, and that he had given her renewed life. Although she wasn't learned in scriptures, she was experienced in Dzogchen, and also practiced the *bodhicitta* teachings. She chanted the *mantra* of great compassion, *Om mani padme hung*, three hundred million times in her life. If one does one hundred million recitations of a mantra, counting each mantra with a rosary, it's called a *toong-jor*. She had done that three times in her life—three hundred million recitations of the mantra of great compassion, the mantra of Chenrezig, *Om mani padme hung*, practicing loving-kindness meditation.

My grandmother advised me that since I was of a gentle nature it would be very appropriate for me to follow my mother's ways, rather than emulating my father. She further exhorted me to find a qualified bodhisattva-lama to teach, instruct, and train me, and to strive to become as enlightened as that lama himself—for that is what the Buddha taught.

For three years I tended the family's animals and performed other similar chores. I didn't study anything, but I kept thinking about this lama whose name I had heard. During this time, when I was five, my mother and grandmother took me to the nearby Sakyapa monastery, where they cut my hair and gave me a refuge name. At eight I was enrolled in the monastery. There were about one hundred monks, practitioners, and lamas in that monastery in Kham. The head lama's name was Jamyang Khenpa Tapkye; he was my distant uncle.

EARLY YEARS AT THE MONASTERY

As my relative, Jamyang Khenpa Tapkye took an interest in me. I was immediately taught to read and write, which came easily to me. Not every boy had such an opportunity. To stay at that monastery the young novices had to beg for their food on a daily alms round in the local villages. I still have scars on my legs from the huge Tibetan mastiffs, fierce guard dogs, that bit me when I went from door to door begging for *tsampa*, dried and roasted barley flour, which is Tibet's staple food. When the young novices were naughty, they would be beaten and forced to sit outside all night without protection from the cold. It was a harsh life.

At the age of about ten my job was to take care of the sheep that belonged to the monastery estate, sometimes staying in the monastery and sometimes shepherding the animals out in the wilds. When it was sunny I would stay outside, very relaxed, feeling very happy, just watching the sheep munching the grass. But sometimes it was raining and freezing cold, with hail and wind, and I was without shelter. Moreover, I couldn't see the sheep who were lost in the mist and ravines. I had to chase them everywhere in order to collect them and bring them back at night. I knew exactly how many there were. I recognized each of their faces and called them each by name.

In the spring and brief summer there was a profusion of bright wild-flowers and all kinds of birds singing. Kham was very beautiful at that time of year. The rest of the time the weather was much colder and severe. I well remember those idyllic summer days of my childhood when the weather was lovely and I was totally delighted, sitting outside in the sun, completely at ease and relaxed, while the sheep munched grass and I gazed up at the intense turquoise blue sky and simply let my mind be. That was the natural, unfabricated beginning of my meditational development.

Sometimes the birds would be chattering, and some thoughts began coming to mind, like: What am I doing here, listening to the birds? Why am I here? Grandmother told me that the only worthwhile thing is to practice and realize the holy Dharma, yet although I have joined the monastery it seems that now I am just being a shepherd. How can I follow the teachings and meet an authentic lama, rather than just be a shepherd in ragged hand-me-down robes, whiling away his time in the pastures?

Mustering my courage, I told my mother that I wanted to learn from a real lama, get genuine spiritual teachings, and find out what the holy Dharma was really all about. Then I left the monastery and went to another valley, where lived a very great high lama named Lama Rigdzin Jampel Dorje. This lama was a truly enlightened master, a *mahasiddha* who had realized the unity of the lineage teachings of Mahamudra and Dzogpa Chenpo.

When I was about twelve, I began and completed the five hundred preliminary practices or *ngondro*, under the personal guidance of this great lama. Then I requested and received from Jampel Dorje detailed teachings on the inseparability of *shamatha* meditation and *vipashyana* meditation practice. I applied these Vajrayana meditation instructions in the Mahamudra style, according to the Practice Lineage. This practice included the renowned four *yogas* of Mahamudra—one-pointedness, simplicity, one taste, and beyond-meditation—which are further elucidated in the three-fold formula of nonmeditation, nonartifice (beyond action and inaction), and nondistraction.

I slowly began noticing that it seemed very difficult to really progress in spiritual practice without a firm basis of understanding in the general teachings of *sutra* and *tantra*, and particularly the precious bodhicitta. It is said, "To meditate without learning is like trying to climb a mountain without eyes; to have learning without meditation is like trying to climb a mountain without hands and feet." Rigdzin Jampel Dorje agreed. So I began to study with an important *khenpo* at the monastery, an erudite and spiritually accomplished abbot-professor. I had to learn, and recite from memory before the monastic assembly, countless prayers, *sadhanas*, scriptures, and commentaries—a huge undertaking.

I studied the three vows of the three vehicles, including the *pratimoksha* vows or vows of personal liberation from the Vinaya, the bodhisattva commitments, and the tantric *samayas*. I studied the *Bodhicaryavatara* of the Indian Mahayana master Shantideva,

the bodhicitta teachings on mind training (attitudinal transformation), or Lojong, of Atisha, and countless other relative and general teachings of the Buddhadharma, according to the sutras and
commentarial literature comprising the scriptures of the Buddhist
tradition. I memorized *The Thirteen Great Texts*. Later I studied in
depth the Middle Way philosophy of Nagarjuna, Madhyamika
dialectics, epistemology, logic, the *Prajnaparamita* literature, the *Five
Ornaments* of Asanga, Vasubandhu's *Abhidharmakosha*, and so on.
Eventually I studied the entire *Tripitaka*, encompassed in the Tibetan canonical collection called the *Kangyur* in one hundred and
eight large volumes, and also the detailed commentaries by the
Indian and Tibetan *panditas* in the even larger collection known as
the *Tangyur*. In this way, combined with actual practice, I mastered
the three *yanas*, including both sutras and tantras—all the teachings of Lord Buddha.

Being intensely motivated, I assiduously pursued that schol-
arly training. Under the extraordinary master Rigdzin Jampel Dorje
and my khenpo, I undertook the traditional twelve-year *acharya* or
khenpo training, combined with the meditation and yogic training of the nonsectarian Rimé Practice Lineage, until I was twenty-
four. I studied all the teachings needed to become a khenpo, an
abbot and a professor, and undertook all the Mahayana and
Vajrayana practices and solitary retreats that went along with them.
I still remember what a small and lonely boy I was then, in a region where I didn't know anyone, and how various people used
to make fun of me. I also gratefully remember my selfless teacher's
incredible kindness and unstinting generosity while I pursued all
those studies and practices for over a dozen years.

RECEIVING THE PITH-INSTRUCTIONS

When I was eighteen, I received the profound and unique, secret
teachings on the essential nature of mind, the pith-instructions of
Longchen Nyingthig, the very heart essence of the Dzogchen teachings. I received these precious esoteric teachings on the view, meditation, and action of Dzogpa Chenpo from the reincarnation (*tulku*)
of my grandmother's guru—teachings that elucidate the ultimate
meaning of Buddhadharma and *rigpa*, innate buddha-mind,
according to the classification of ground, path, and fruition, a triad

considered ultimately one and inseparable. I soon attained unshakable inner conviction and certainty regarding this natural Great Perfection, the nondual Dzogchen teachings of primordial purity and spontaneous presence embodied in the practices of Trekchod—Cutting Through, and Togal—Transcendence.

Nyoshul Lungtok Tenpai Nyima, Patrul Rinpoche's successor, had died years before. His tulku had been reborn, enthroned, and educated by the disciples of his exalted predecessor, including the peerless Khenpo Ngakga. It was this tulku, named Nyoshul Lungtok Shedrup Tenpai Nyima, who introduced me to the nature of mind while transmitting these teachings. He became my root guru. I received my name from him, and from the Nyoshul Monastery where we lived together, in the outlying districts around the region of the great Nyingma monastery of Kathok. From these lamas I inherited all the teachings of Longchenpa and Jigme Lingpa. I memorized the entire *Seven Treasures* of Longchenpa, as well as both of Longchenpa's renowned trilogies, *The Trilogy of Natural Ease* and *The Trilogy of the Inherent Freedom of Mind*, and Jigme Lingpa's revered *Yonten Dzod, The Treasury of Enlightened Qualities*, which explains all the nine yanas according to the Nyingma tradition of Buddhadharma. I was completely happy.

Tulku Shedrup Tenpai Nyima transmitted the *Nyengyud Men Ngag Chenmo*, the whispered oral pith-instructions of Dzogpa Chenpo, to me. Tulku Shedrup Tenpai Nyima was the principal disciple of the great Khenpo Ngakga: Ngakgi Wangpo, a crazy-wise Dzogchen master still renowned today—a visionary Togal master and an incarnation of the Indian Dzogchen patriarch Vimalamitra. When I was very young, I met Khenpo Ngakga and received certain transmissions from him. I was too young to really study in depth under Khenpo Ngakga, so I gradually received Khenpo Ngakga's teachings personally from Nyoshul Lungtok Shedrup Tenpai Nyima.

Khenpo Ngakga had extraordinary dignity and charisma, and was an incredible presence. Simply to enter his room overawed one's self-centered thoughts and concepts, effortlessly opening up the selfless, spacious expanse of rigpa. Even though I was but a youth, I still remember thinking gratefully at the time, "So this is what the authentic presence of a true Buddhist master is actually like. Anyone would be totally amazed and inspired by such natural splendor and spiritual prowess. How fortunate to meet a living Buddha in this very world!"

This greatly renowned Khenpo Ngakga was famous for many reasons. He once sat for three years on one meditation seat, without going anywhere. When this grand lama did a three-year meditation retreat, he was in a translucent state of rigpa called *zangtal* throughout the entire period; nobody could see a shadow fall from his body for three years. This is absolutely true.

While Khenpo Ngakga was in this meditation, on auspicious days like the tenth of every month—Guru Rinpoche's lunar holiday, and the fifteenth—the day of the full moon, the eight auspicious signs would appear on Ngakga's body, because his body was the actual *nirmanakaya*, the *rupakaya*, the manifestation on earth of the Buddha. Khenpo Ngakga had such inconceivable qualities that any of them sounds hard to believe, but so many of the lamas who were his students achieved enlightenment that everybody extols Khenpo Ngakga to the skies. Jatral Rinpoche and Bairo Tulku Rinpoche in Nepal are Khenpo Ngakga's last great, living, personal disciples.

The Dzogchen tradition states that every one hundred years an enlightened Dzogchen master is emanated from the heart of Vimalamitra to fulfill the Buddha's intent in this world. In the nineteenth century it was Jamyang Khyentse Wangpo, and in the last generation it was Khenpo Ngakga. Khenpo Ngakga had thousands of realized disciples, but Nyoshul Lungtok Shedrup Tenpai Nyima, my root guru, was his Dharma heir, the lineage holder of the special Dzogchen pith-instructions called *Nyengyud Men Ngag Chenmo, The Aural Lineage Pith-Instructions of the Heart Essence*. This is my special lineage and teaching, the experiential teaching (*nyongtri*) based on these oral pith-instructions of Nyingthig, the heart essence of omniscient Longchenpa and Jigme Lingpa, the quintessence of the innate Great Perfection, Dzogpa Chenpo. This is a lineage transmission only whispered to one disciple at a time, never to a group. It is considered extremely rare and precious. I too have passed it on to a very few close personal lama-disciples.

The lineage holders and masters of this particular teaching were all enlightened, totally realized *siddhas* with incredible spiritual qualities, but these days lamas like me are a mere shadow of such spiritual luminaries. Those masters of the rainbow-light body didn't even cast shadows; now people with physical infirmities like Nyoshul Khenpo pretend to transmit such transcendent teaching —how absurd! The elixir of liberating pith-instructions in this unique lineage is like the fresh breath of the wisdom *dakinis*. The lion's roar of the Dharma has been proclaimed by great snow-lion-like *yogis* in the land of Tibet for thousands of years, but these days there are just a few dogs like Nyoshul Khenpo barking. And not only that, they shamelessly go here and there to every country in the world, barking, eating others' food, and kicking up a ruckus— how utterly laughable!

I spent several years at Kathok Monastery, one of the six main Nyingmapa monasteries. Kathok was called in Tibetan, Kathok Dorje Den, meaning Kathok Bodhgaya or Kathok the vajra-seat of enlightenment. This seven-hundred-year-old *gompa* in Kham is renowned as the second Bodhgaya. It is reported that one hundred thousand yogis attained the rainbow-light body there. Another tale recalls the fabled yellow sky of Kathok, where so many fully ordained *bhikshus* lived that the sky continuously reflected the bright yellow hue of their formal monastic robes.

At Kathok Gompa my own lamas were twelve great tulkus; eight spiritually accomplished, learned khenpos, the kind of khenpos (unlike many today) who knew everything and had memorized the entire Kangyur and many of the commentaries too; and five enlightened lamas who were neither tulkus nor khenpos, but had achieved great attainments through their own spiritual efforts, while remaining humble practitioners and staunch pillars of the *sangha*.

After receiving the significant pith-instruction transmission from Tulku Shedrup Tenpai Nyima, I did a one-year solitary retreat in a cave, practicing *tummo*, mystic inner-heat yoga, and concentrating on those aural pith-instruction teachings. I further pursued my studies until my mid-twenties. I practiced tummo in the snowy wilderness until the falling snow melted around me. During another period of intensive practice I lived for a time like a wild animal in the forest, uninhibitedly practicing *rushen*, the Dzogchen preliminary practices, with several other yogis under the guidance of my guru. I still remember what that was like, living freely and uninhibitedly, beyond all conceptual restraints and social conventions—just like the mahasiddhas of old! It was a wonderful period of spiritual practice. *Emaho!*

I practiced the tantric Prajnaparamita sadhanas called Chöd or Cutting Ego, meditating all night in terrifying cemeteries and charnel grounds, offering my body to the hungry ghosts and karmic creditors. Other periods I spent meditating alone on windswept mountaintops and in caves consecrated by the lineage masters of old, or on pilgrimage to sacred sites and Shangri-la-like hidden valleys where the patriarchs and matriarchs of Vajrayana Buddhism had meditated, where I made offerings and supported virtuous and worthwhile spiritual activities. I completed the training in the Six Yogas of Naropa and Mahamudra according to the Kagyu system, as well as the Sakyapa Lamdray—Path and Fruition, and Korday Yermay—The Inseparability of Samsara and Nirvana, and the anuttara yoga tantra Kalachakra teachings. My lama acknowledged that I completed all these various practices, encountered the yidam deities, and received blessings, transmissions, and empowerments directly from them, just like the root and lineage masters of the past.

Then I traveled, receiving teachings and Vajrayana transmissions from two dozen other enlightened masters, whom I consider my root lamas, from all the different traditions and lineages extant in Tibet. By that time I knew what I was after and where to find it. I practiced and accomplished these teachings, thus becoming a nonsectarian Rimé lama, heir to all the sacred teachings of the Eight Great Chariots of Buddhism in Tibet, which are now subsumed within the four main Tibetan sects: Nyingma, Kagyu, Sakya, and Gelug.

ESCAPE FROM TIBET

My colleagues and I had to escape from Tibet in 1959, because of the Chinese invasion. Any monks, nuns, and lamas who were caught were disrobed, imprisoned, humiliated, beaten, and killed or tortured mercilessly. Religious practice in Tibet during the sixties and seventies was considered a reactionary political crime, punishable by death. I lost touch with all who remained behind, including the vestiges of my family. I would not be reunited with my surviving brothers and sisters until a visit to eastern Tibet in 1992.

In India I requested and received complete teachings and transmissions from many great Tibetan masters, including Padmasambhava's incarnate regent, H.H. Dudjom Rinpoche; Dilgo Khyentse Rinpoche—Manjushri in person; and the living Buddha, H.H. the Sixteenth Gyalwa Karmapa. Later, these same lamas, as well as others, including Tai Situ Rinpoche, Pema Norbu Rinpoche, Sakya Trichen, and Dzogchen Rinpoche, asked me to be khenpo or abbot-professor at their monasteries, in order to educate sangha members and train khenpos in dialectic colleges.

I still pray constantly to those twenty-five root masters who gave me everything that I know and have. For even if one knows hundreds of thousands of excellent people—or, for that matter, hundreds of thousands of evil people—one's *tsawai lama* or root guru is the most important person in one's life. Actually, what truly astounds me the most is not my teachers, but the teachings of the natural Great Perfection, Dzogchen: that is the really marvelous, magical, and most inconceivable surprise in my experience, and the thing I am most grateful for. I am inexpressibly grateful to my teachers for the teachings they gave me. I try to do all I can to repay their kindness by passing it on to others, wherever I have been over the years. For I truly believe that it is this, and this alone, that is most profoundly beneficial.

I lived in India for twenty-five years by myself, without accumulating anything, just one old man alone, sometimes walking around in red Tibetan-style lama clothes, sometimes in old orange or yellow *sadhu* robes or simple wraps. Sometimes I gave Dharma talks inside monasteries. I also stayed sometimes with sadhus in Rishikesh and Haridwar, along the Ganges, in ashrams, huts, lean-tos, under trees, wherever the descent of dusk found me. So many different dream-like experiences! Sometimes I was exalted and quite comfortable, more often I was bereft and poverty-stricken. Yet the inexhaustible wealth of inner truth and peace that is the Dharma always sustained me well. Sometimes I gave empowerments to great assemblies of people, including dozens of tulkus and lamas, where they put a golden initiation vase in my hand and I placed it on the heads of thousands of monks. At other times I was utterly poor, living hand-to-mouth on the streets in Calcutta, wandering around with my hand out begging for pennies. So many unexpected ups and downs, who can describe them? Life is like that, full of unexpected twists and turns—illusory, impermanent, ungovernable, and unstable. And in the end, we all die. What a spectacle!

So many different experiences, memories, and reflections—some good and some bad—just like different kinds of dreams. One night in 1959 I was with about seventy people who were escaping together from Tibet, and a few thousand Chinese soldiers were in the surrounding mountains, searching for fugitives in the darkness. The soldiers suddenly opened fire, and machine gun bullets and tracers flew everywhere. Of the seventy in my party, only five could be found alive the next day. I don't know what happened to the rest. Our small band of five continued on foot through the high Himalayan passes to India, following in the footsteps of the Dalai Lama, seeking refuge in Assam, Bhutan, Darjeeling, and Kalimpong—wherever food, shelter, and political asylum were to be found.

I then lived in the lowlands as a refugee for years, in exile from the Land of Snows, huddled with others in crowded refugee camps and steamy trains, collecting alms in hot and dusty Indian streets. Some years later I unexpectedly found myself riding across vast oceans in jet airplanes, and coasting up and down the length of giant needle-shaped skyscrapers in boxcar-like air-conditioned elevators in the great capitals of the modern world, sleeping in both grand hotels and on the rugs and couches of modern living rooms, eating in restaurants and outdoors on sunny patios, being served like a king.

In the early seventies, I seemed to have a stroke and almost died. Some think I was poisoned in a restaurant in Kalimpong. My nervous system was traumatized; I was a complete invalid for several years. Before that, I had given vast and profound teachings and cycles of empowerments to many people, including monks, lamas, tulkus, and laypersons, all over the Himalayan region. Afterwards, I could not see very well, I was lame, my hands shook, and I was expected to die. During that difficult time I was cared for in Kangyur Rinpoche's monastery in Darjeeling. Kangyur Rinpoche and his family graciously cared for me. I always think of them with profound gratitude and respect. Lama Sonam Tobgyal from Riwoché Gompa was my faithful attendant for six years during that period, in India and later in Europe.

The grand yogi-master of Bhutan, Lopon Sonam Zangpo, suggested to me that if I would take a wife and undertake longevity practices my health would improve. (I had been a monk until this time.) The old and venerable yogi, who was the father of Trinley Norbu Rinpoche's late wife, arranged for me to marry Damcho Zangmo, who proved to be a perfectly suitable long-life consort and wife. We have been together since then.

Some time later I was brought to Switzerland for medical treatment. I stayed a couple of years with my Tibetan followers in the large Tibetan community there, then spent seven or eight years in retirement in the Nyingma center in the Dordogne Valley in southwestern France, teaching only occasionally. For four years I lived and taught in the Chanteloube three-year retreat center there, after which—in 1984—my wife, Damcho-la, came from Bhutan to join me.

Since that time my health has improved and I have been more active, teaching all around the world, in both East and West, invited by centers of many different sects and lineages. Damcho-la and I have made two visits to Tibet: once with H.H. Khyentse Rinpoche and an entourage in 1990, and again with Penor Rinpoche in 1992, when I met my remaining family members. I am currently working to rebuild my three monasteries and to construct several small new hospitals in Kham. Damcho-la and I make our home at her house in Thimpu, the capital of Bhutan, the last remaining independent Buddhist country in the Himalayas.

LIKE A DREAM, LIKE A MIRAGE

Isn't life like a movie or a dream, like a series of dreams within a vast, dream-like mirage? How to possibly remember all the different scenes that inevitably transpired from the time that I was an illiterate little scamp in Kham until now, when I am a talkative old vagabond with white hair, glasses, and wrinkles? What a surprise! Old and bent already. What a spectacle! A dim-sighted aged Tibetan tourist peering around at foreign lands. *Emaho!* Marvelous! Wonderful!

How to explain the infinite vagaries of experience, except by considering it all as the workings of the ineluctable law of cause and effect, karma? And who is creating this karma, who except ourselves? When we recognize that we create our own karma, and are therefore responsible for our own experience, both good and bad, wanted and unwanted, doesn't this penetrating insight free us from resentment and frustration, instilling a sense of freedom and responsibility, as well as compassion for those who suffer from a lack of such awareness?

It is probably not really meaningful for me to talk about this life, but it does remind me of all the sacred Dharma I've enjoyed—a genuine cause for rejoicing in these turbulent times. The Dharma comes in many forms, but all are endowed with the single savor of great peace.

Actually I am just an insignificant person; my only interest is in service, assisting others, and helping preserve and spread the Dharma. I have absolutely no special work left to do, but I do feel that since the Buddhadharma has helped me so much in this life, I am very happy to help by offering my own experience to anybody who is interested in the Dharma. I hope that in the future the sublime Dharma, the liberating teachings, will flourish and benefit beings everywhere, whoever those beings might be. I am not a translator, so I can't talk to Western people in their own language; I merely try to represent the Dharma in every way, as best I can.

I am delighted to see that many people in the West also appreciate how significant, beneficial, and genuinely helpful the Dharma is. That is the only thing that I really know in life: the excellent virtues of the Buddhadharma. Therefore I rejoice to see that other people also feel the same way, and I know that if they apply it in actual practice, with introspection, they will be able to extract the benefit from these profound and meaningful teachings. Wouldn't it be great to realize that unique, panaceaic self-knowledge which liberates and frees one and all, rather than continuing in the endless pursuit of infinite forms of knowledge, none of which are of much ultimate benefit either to oneself or others?

Even on the subways of Paris and London I have seen people—who aren't Buddhists—whose spiritual faculties are sufficiently keen to enable them to immediately apprehend the true import of the nondual Dharma, if only it could be introduced to them by a qualified teacher. When the moment of Dzogchen arrives, that's it!

It is not a matter of culture or study, but of one's spiritual affinity and karmic ripeness.

I am heartened these days to encounter Western Dharma practitioners who sincerely seek genuine experiential knowledge, and are unsatisfied with mere platitudes and external religious events. These are people who are willing and eager to plunge deep within themselves, to study and practice the teachings, making sacrifices even, in order to exert themselves in the cultivation of spiritual awareness. Isn't the Dharma everywhere? Is there anywhere else to seek and discover it, except within oneself, within one's own heart-mind?

As Jigme Lingpa's supreme *Longchen Nyingthig Guru Yoga, The Tigle Gyachen* terma sadhana begins:

> No Buddhas and no beings, beyond both existence and
>   nonexistence,
> Intrinsic awareness-itself is the absolute guru, the ultimate
>   truth.
> By resting naturally, beyond fixation, in that inherently free
>   and perfect innate bodhi-mind,
> I take refuge and actualize bodhicitta.

A *vidyadhara* or rigpa master like Rigdzin Jigme Lingpa actually realized Buddhahood through the way of Dzogpa Chenpo. Then, although he had never studied much, because his wisdom chakra blossomed he could spontaneously write invaluable commentaries, sing glorious *dohas*, reveal the precious *termas* of Longchen Nyingthig through mystic revelation, and teach widely, illuminating our way even today, three centuries later.

I myself have not attained Buddhahood, and I don't know where I will be in the future, neither in this very life nor in the next. But that really doesn't matter, not at all! Whatever happens, happens. There is absolutely nothing to be concerned about. I simply feel gratitude to my teachers, to the teachings, and to the Buddha, and I wish that all beings can participate in these blessings, these virtues, which actually belong to everyone without exception. Therefore, I continuously pray that all beings may make this auspicious connection, through whatever means are appropriate and beneficial.

May all beings awaken in the light of the innate Great Perfection and actualize perfect freedom, peace, and fulfillment!

Sarva mangalam! May everything be perfectly auspicious, and may there be peace in this world and throughout the entire universe.

Primordial Buddha Samantabhadra with consort (yab-yum), in the Mandala of One Hundred Peaceful and Wrathful Deities. Photo courtesy of the author.

Teachings

2   Basic Buddhadharma

A Teaching in the Kingdom of Bhutan

Translated by Lama Matthieu Ricard

Many people now receive a modern education, sharpen their intelligence, and acquire a lot of knowledge. They open their minds to the vast field of knowledge of science and other disciplines. At the same time, many of them, after completing their studies, wonder, "What is the Dharma?"

Although they live in a Buddhist country, many young men and women here have not had a chance find out what the Dharma is about and what use they can make of it. For many the Dharma is to receive initiations and blessings from lamas, offer butter lamps, circumambulate *stupas* and temples, wear monastic robes, and other similar external activities. To do this is indeed meritorious and indicates the general interest people have for religion, but these are mere branches of the Dharma; they are not the main point. To have a ritual vase placed upon one's head is indeed a blessing, but that is not what we call the holy Dharma.

What then is the need for the Dharma? To answer this question, we must first look around and reflect upon our situation in this world. If we do so without blinding ourselves to reality, we find one main point, common to all sentient beings: suffering and dissatisfaction.

Everyone suffers in one way or the other. A leader has leader problems, and a worker has worker problems. When you see a leader passing in the street, you may think, "He has reached to a high rank, he has a comfortable house, a nice car, and so on. He must be a happy person." But that is not at all the case. That leader suffers. He worries about losing his position, or he has too much work, or he is tormented by the desire to become a world leader, or his family is unhappy, and so on. The worker has to run here and there, gets the most tedious work, and is paid little. Even the president of United States is worried about lack of approval, of not succeeding in bringing the whole world under his influence, and so on. Even if he could do so, he would then be tormented by the need to keep things under control.

Is there an ultimate solution to these problems? In the ordinary world there is none. You may think that if you give $1 million to a beggar, that will bring him happiness. But not at all! If he gets $1 million he may appreciate having enough food and clothes, but then he will want $2 million! No one is ever satisfied for long with worldly wealth and power. This is because worldly people are confused; they do not know what is genuine wealth, authentic power, real lasting fulfillment. As Nagarjuna said, "Contentment is true wealth."

A rich person can never quite be happy either. He will be obsessed at first with acquiring his wealth, then with guarding and increasing it. Moreover, how many people are bedridden in hospitals, dying of famine, or in wars? How many families are torn apart by quarrels, and eventually death? That may not happen to you right now, but who knows?

Although the modern world has developed science and technology to an unimaginable extent, as yet there is no machine, no trick, no pill, that can remove suffering and generate lasting happiness. Yet to remove suffering is precisely the goal of the sacred Dharma—and not just the symptoms of suffering, but the very cause of it.

How can the teachings effect such a noble end? The real reason beings suffer is not to be found outside, but within themselves. We suffer because of attachment, desire, anger, repulsion, pride, jealousy, and confusion—all sorts of mental poisons. Therefore, true Dharma is work on the heart and mind.

Mind is very powerful: it can create both suffering and happiness, heaven and hell. If, with the help of spiritual teachings and practice, you subdue your inner poisons, your conflicting emotions, and transcend small-minded ignorance, then nothing can ever affect your happiness. But as long as these poisons remain anchored in your mind, nowhere in the world will you find your greatest desire, happiness. Wherever you may go, your own projections and confusion follow.

To work on the mind is a very vast subject; in fact, it is the subject of the entire Buddhadharma. In essence, the main reason the mind generates its confusing passions and intense emotions is our strong clinging to *I*, *me*, and *mine*. Because of that clinging, we suffer when we do not obtain all that the *I* wants, and we suffer by experiencing what the *I* does not want.

It is through meditating over and again on the illusory and insubstantial nature of mind, of ego, of self, that we slowly can dissolve ego-clinging. Among all the methods to achieve this result, the deepest one is the meditation on bodhicitta—unselfish love and compassion. To be full of love for all sentient beings and to consider others more important than ourselves is the very root of Dharma, combining wisdom and compassion.

We must also have faith, devotion, and confidence. Faith does not mean to blindly believe in religion because our lama told us so. Faith is a genuine, joyful appreciation of the boundless qualities of enlightenment and enlightened beings, such as the Buddha, or any enlightened being, male or female. It is the recognition of the difference between a fully awakened, compassionate Buddha, and an ordinary, troubled human being. This difference is simply that a Buddha's mind is illumined and free of delusion, while an ordinary being's mind is obscured. To acquire complete certainty in this difference, and to deeply yearn to acquire the Buddha's awareness wisdom, is what we call faith.

The infinite Buddhas of the past, present, and future are appropriate objects of faith. If, in this modern age, you give your faith to the Lotus-Born Guru, Padmasambhava, you will receive his blessings. He made the promise that his compassion for the beings of this dark age will be swifter than that of any other Buddha. As he said, "I am always nearby, at the very threshold of your devotion."

Especially in this country, Bhutan, one can see many proofs of Guru Rinpoche's blessings. If Guru Rinpoche left the imprint of his feet, of his hands, of his body, in Paro Taksang, in Tango, in Bumthang Kuje, it is not because Guru Rinpoche did not find any other work to do, or just to amuse himself with miracle working. It was simply to leave visible signs of his infinite spiritual prowess, to help sentient beings by inspiring their faith and devotion, and to lend credence to the truth of his word. If anyone here would confirm for him or herself the truth of the Buddha's message, he or she would in that instant be equal to Padmasambhava.

Appreciate the value and opportunity of this human existence. Give it meaning, both for yourself and for others, by unfolding all that is within you. Have faith, compassion, and devotion. Find happiness within: transform your mind and the outer world naturally transforms itself into immutable, deathless bliss.

DEVELOPING THE RIGHT ATTITUDE

This first requirement in order to be a suitable recipient of the sacred teachings is to have the right attitude, to be able receive it in a proper way. We should remember that the essential point of the Dharma is to affect the heart and mind. If the point of Dharma is to deal with the heart and mind, then it is appropriate to prepare ourselves in a relevant fashion. To prepare our mind we should check our attitude: Why are we coming to receive the teachings? What do we expect from them? What is our motivation for receiving the teachings? When we receive the teachings, it is more important to reflect on the meaning of what we are going to receive than the words themselves. The words may be very beautiful, learned, and poetic, but that is only the superficial aspect of the teachings. What is important is their significance, their actual meaning.

To be able to grasp the meaning, we must first turn our minds inward, check our motivation, and become receptive to the teachings, by opening our hearts and minds. It is very important to turn our minds inward. Until now, due to ignorance, we have been wandering around since beginningless time in *samsara*, our mind constantly projected toward external phenomena. Therefore, the first step is to turn within, check our attitude, and become aware in the here and now of what the mind is doing, of what attitudes it has—in general, to be aware of the workings of our own inner mind.

We may consider ourselves Buddhists. In a way that is good, because the Buddhist teachings are extremely vast and blessed. However, we should not have a limited and narrow view regarding that. What does it mean to think of ourselves as Buddhists? Is it merely another way for our egotism to help us feel superior to other people elsewhere in the world? Are we really Buddhists, bodhisattvas, spiritual practitioners—or perhaps just following our ancestors, without more than a superficial resemblance to true followers of the omniscient Buddha? We should have a very open mind, and consider—know, even—all the other different Dharmas, the different religions and philosophies in this world. Even this knowledge would also be quite limited, because there is not only this world but billions of other universes. For each of these world systems, out of the compassion of the Buddha, there are liberating teachings.

Similarly, as the number of beings is infinite, so also are the methods to bring sentient beings to the ultimate goal. All these teachings assist in realizing the absolute truth, the natural state of all phenomena, ultimate knowledge. But since different beings have different capacities, inclinations, and aspirations, there are different means to lead them to ultimate understanding. Therefore, do not have such a narrow point of view as to consider only your own religion, or even only your universe, but try to be very open and realize there are infinitely various beings, countless different approaches and teachings leading to the ultimate goal. We should have a very vast and spacious attitude and be open to all forms of the truth, all the different paths that can bring beings to the ultimate understanding.

The significance of having such an open mind is to realize that there are so many different manifestations of the Buddhas to meet the needs of each and every sentient being. The enlightened ones can manifest in so many different forms, in so many different realms of existence, displaying according to the *dharmakaya, sambhogakaya,* or *nirmanakaya* dimensions of buddha-mind. All these ways to benefit beings are ultimately designed to help us realize the ultimate nature of mind.

THE POWER OF DELUSION

In all these infinite universes and among all sentient beings, the common factor is that they all have a mind, awareness, some form of consciousness which distinguishes them from inanimate matter. And for each of them, the mind has fallen under the power of delusion. The best way to help beings is to clear away the delusion through the different skillful methods and teachings leading to the realization of the absolute nature of mind.

Once we become aware of the immeasurable sweep of time and space, the infinite numbers of universes, beings, and Buddhas, then our own life seems as short as a lightning flash in the sky. Not only our life, but this particular universe is just like one brief instant, even if it has been in existence for billions of years; for this is like one short second compared with the infinity of the entire cosmos. This larger perspective will lead us to vivid and very present awareness of the impermanence and shortness of our life. Moreover, in the light of infinity, we will realize the shortcomings and limitations of this conditioned, samsaric life. Upon opening ourselves to these vast infinities, we become vividly aware of our own limitations, of the vicissitudes of conditioned existence, of impermanence—how short is our life and time. We see how narrow, constricted, and shortsighted our usual self-centered concerns are, in the light of the infinite, shimmering void.

If we look at the rays of the sun, we can sometimes see a tiny particle of dust. According to the Buddhist way of looking at matter, if we take one fortieth the size of this very tiny particle of dust, we arrive at the basic atom or molecule. It is stated that on this minute particle there are infinite universes, and in each of these universes there are six realms—there are hells, there are realms equivalent to human beings, there are god realms, and so forth. There is also suffering.

If we try to see the root of that suffering, we will see that it comes from the distinction between the deluded mind and the undeluded mind. All these universes, and all these various perceptions of the different realms in these universes, arise out of the mind's delusion. The purpose of the Dharma is to find out exactly what is the undeluded mind; what is our true nature. This is what we call buddha-nature, or the Buddha within.

It all boils down to the distinctions between delusion and non-delusion, between attachment and nonattachment—between suffering and absolute peace, freedom, enlightenment. This is why, when we start receiving the teachings, we should check our own attitude, inquiring into our present state of mind. What is it doing? What does it feel? Is it distracted, dull, unfocussed, or vividly present and alert? Is it prepared to receive these profound teachings? Everything is going to revolve around, or converge upon, the inner understanding of the mind.

In the same way as there are infinite universes and beings, we ourselves have been going through numberless rebirths, states of existence, countless bodies, innumerable lives, and so forth. Again and again we are going to be reborn. Why is that? Because our mind-stream is totally conditioned by, and at the mercy of, the winds of *karma* and *klesha*—obscuring emotions. All of this originated from that deluded mind.

It is said that samsara is beginningless, but has an end—in nirvana, enlightenment; and that nirvana has a beginning—enlightenment—but no end. Just as one cannot assign a beginning point to samsara, one cannot assign a beginning point to the mind. The mind has forever been accomplishing its self-appointed work of generating endless thoughts, one following after another, chains of thought that actually shackle us. Even in one day we cannot count the number of thoughts we have, for they are numberless. When we may try to meditate once in a while, we are often amazed at the amount of thoughts that assail us, as if there is more thinking when we sit and meditate than under more ordinary circumstances. But this is wrong; it is simply because when we meditate we become aware for the first time of how many thoughts we always have, of how out of control our minds are, and of how thought enslaves us.

It is precisely because of the work of these thoughts, because of following these thoughts, that we engage in words and physical actions, and reap karma by continuously doing so. The strength of that karma perpetuates the cycle of birth and death and keeps us continually circling around, taking rebirth again and again, on the wheel of samsara. All of this basically occurs due to the mind's delusion. That is why the main purpose of these Dharma teachings will be to find out what is the nature of the nondeluded mind, as well as how the deluded mind works.

Not only ourselves, but innumerable beings are circling help-lessly in the vicious cycle of samsara. They are enduring so many kinds of suffering, for the same reason. All their suffering comes from the delusion of the mind. If we want to find a remedy for that, there is no other remedy than truth, which is embodied in the Dharma—any other method will fail. This is also why all religions are aimed at understanding the work of the mind, freeing the mind from its delusion, which they may do either directly or indirectly. Of course there are some aspects of religion that do not explicitly state, "This is specifically to work on your mind, to benefit your mind." But actually, whether it says it directly or indirectly, the purpose of all religions is to free the mind of its delusion and find peace and happiness.

Just as all rivers on the earth come to the ocean—although some go straight to the ocean, while others go in a winding manner, or join along the way with other rivers—likewise, whether it is stated or not, the true basic aim of any dharma, Buddhist or non-Bud-dhist, is to transform the heart and mind and ultimately reach free-dom from delusion, true transcendence. It is not that all religions are exactly the same, but this remains the crucial point of the liber-ating Dharma. One sometimes finds apparent contradictions in the outer expressions and manifestations of different world religions. For instance, in the Buddhist religion we say that it is a very seri-ous sin to kill, to take a life, while in some aspects of the Muslim religion, and Hinduism too, goats are sacrificed. But there are ac-tually more similarities than differences. If we examine all the reli-gions of the world we see that, and we should be able to harmo-nize with their truly essential principles.

All these various expressions and manifestations of ways people are seeking their highest good arise from the mind. The mind's delusion is extremely powerful and has a very strong grasp on us. It is not easy to dissolve that delusion of the mind, but that is the principal goal of Dharma practice. The whole difference between ignorance and enlightenment, between freedom and bondage, is whether the mind is deluded or not.

Ordinary life is like a dream, a mirage, an echo. What we nor-mally give such importance to, and so readily believe in, is all delusional, insubstantial, unreal. It is as easily concocted as our night-time dreams. Therefore, an awakened, realized being, having transcended the mind's delusion, sees our ordinary state of delusion, too, as like a dream, and is not taken in by it. This is one significant reason why he or she can genuinely help guide and liberate us.

What we are living is like one long dream, a longer dream than ordinary sleeping dreams, but whether for ten minutes or our whole lives, the illusory nature of dreams is the same. When we know and experience the long dream of this life, then after we die we will have another long dream—of being born in another state of existence. Thus, one long dream will follow another, as long as delusion remains.

The extraordinary quality of the Buddhadharma is that it gives us the means to recognize that this life is just like a dream, that it lacks true existence, and all of our self-centered samsaric aims are relatively meaningless, senseless, and unproductive—that they have no essence and are without true reality. Not only will we come to realize this, but the Dharma also gives us the chance to see that there is a way to dispel our delusion and, through skillful means, reach the ultimate realization of the buddha-nature, which is total freedom from delusion, perfect freedom and transcendental peace. This is what makes the Dharma the most precious jewel, the jewel of our hearts, because it is the only method that gives us the chance to recognize the delusory nature of the world and, at the same time, moves us beyond that delusion toward true realization.

Let us take the example of our body to understand the power and strength delusion can have. At present, it is very natural for us to have this body; we cherish and cling to it greatly. Our bodily safety and comfort and sense pleasures are one of our main preoccupations, one of the main objects of clinging and attachment. But if we gradually try to discover how this body came into existence, going back to our youth, then to when we were a baby, and finally the seeds of our father and mother, we see that our whole body started from the meeting of these two seeds. And how did that meeting happen? It was by the strength of desire, which itself comes from delusion of past karma. Because of that karmic conditioning or tendency, that desire was there. It creates an impulse to take existence again in conditioned existence. The mind energy gets attached between the white and red seeds of the father and mother; thus a being comes into existence in a body. Then the body grows; consciousness individuates and evolves and becomes attached to it.

The time will again arrive when we meet death. What will happen to the body? It will again dissolve back into nothing, just like when a rainbow disappears in the sky: when it is there, we can see its five colors very vividly, but when it vanishes, it has not descended into the valley, it has not ascended to the top of the mountain—it just disappears. The body to which we cling so much will turn into nothing. Only the consciousness will continue, and it will be propelled again and again by the strength of karma and habitual tendencies and attachments to seek the seeds of a father and mother and perpetuate this cycle of existence. Yet each body we take will, like clay pots, simply be formed from the five elements, and again completely disappear without leaving the slightest trace.

Everything is impermanent. All that is born, dies. By the power of delusion, our bodies successively form and disappear, perpetuating the endless cycle of samsara. What we actually need to find is a teaching that will take us to a state of nondelusion and free us from this vicious cycle. This is why we need to turn our mind inward, attentively check and work on the mind itself whenever we start to listen to or practice the Dharma, because the mind is the main subject of the Buddhist teachings.

If we turn our mind in upon itself to see what it does, there are only three modes of thought the mind can adopt. One is negative thoughts: attachment, hatred, stupidity, and so on. The next mode is positive thoughts: compassion, altruism, kindness, love, aspiration to benefit beings, devotion, and so on. Then there are neutral, indifferent states of thought, such as when we sleep, are complacent or mindless, which have neither negative nor positive aspects. There are no categories of thoughts other than these three classifications.

First we need to dispel the negative thoughts, including attachment, hatred, and ignorance. We do not need to reject the neutral thoughts: we need to transform them and bring them into the Dharma. And we must cultivate and develop the positive thoughts—devotion, renunciation or detachment, and bodhicitta, the enlightened attitude. The practice is to abandon the negative thoughts, words and deeds, transform the neutral ones, and increase the positive.

When we examine negative thoughts, we find there are three: the impulse of grasping, the impulse of rejecting, and ignorance or close-minded mental darkness. If we examine these, we find that desire and hatred are basically caused by mental darkness or ignorance. It means not to see, understand, or realize the true nature of things. Attachment, hatred, grasping, judging, rejecting, and so on, arise due to the lack of awareness of the true nature of mind and phenomena. Knowing that this is the main cause, we must find the remedy for it, the antidote. The antidote comes precisely by cultivating the positive thoughts like devotion, renunciation, and altruism—the beneficial mind of bodhicitta, which selflessly aspires to deliver all beings to Buddhahood.

CULTIVATING BODHICITTA

We need to cultivate bodhicitta as a means for dispelling the basic ignorance that creates negative thoughts. There are many teachings dealing with how to reject negative thoughts and transform neutral thoughts. But since this is such a vast subject, we will only have a few words on the precious bodhicitta, the root of all positive thoughts.

To meditate on bodhicitta, we first need to have a very complete understanding, because this is an infinitely vast subject. Why is that so? Because it deals with the understanding of the universal delusion of all sentient beings in the infinite number of universes. Not only ourselves, but our parents and all sentient beings have been deluded for countless lives, and because of that delusion, they have, without exception, suffered greatly. Therefore, the basic cultivation of bodhicitta requires an understanding of the vastness of the delusion and sufferings of beings. When one becomes aware of the limitless extent of lives and universes where beings fall into delusion and suffering, only then can genuine feelings of compassion, and wishes to free those beings, develop in our mind. Thus, we need to become aware of the extent of delusion and suffering, not to become depressed or pessimistic, but to see things as they are and to bring forth the best for ourselves and all beings everywhere.

What do we mean by bodhicitta? Bodhicitta in Tibetan is *chang-chub*. This word has two basic meanings. First, *chang* means "to purify." In Dharma language we would say "purify the two veils or obscurations." In ordinary language this means to clear all the defects, stains, imperfections, and shortcomings of our mind. When we speak of *chub* it means "to be endowed with" or "to be rich with." This means to develop to the ultimate point all the inherent qualities, or potentialities, in the heart and mind. Therefore, bodhicitta, *chang-chub*, means to clear whatever defects there may be and to develop all possible enlightened qualities. Why do we say bodhicitta or enlightened mind? Because the beginning point is the benighted, deluded mind, and the end point is the enlightened mind. So bodhicitta deals with the purification and the ultimate development of the mind.

When the purification of the mind and the development of all those enlightened qualities reaches its ultimate point—the actualization of all the qualities of the mind and the discarding of all the veils—that state is called the Buddha, or Guru Rinpoche, or Chenrezig, or Avalokiteshvara. It is nothing other than the enlightened state in which all the qualities have been developed; there is no need to be confused by a multitude of forms, for all are of one single essential nature.

So why do we need to meditate on bodhicitta, the enlightened mind? It is because of our condition, our suffering and delusion. When all the delusion has been dispelled, this is the state called "Buddhahood": the state of one who has actualized the ultimate qualities and dispelled all defects. One may proceed from the ordinary deluded state to the enlightened state; this is called "the path." But this enlightened nature is actually within ourselves, for it is our own true nature.

This innate buddha-nature—the fundamental enlightened mind within each of us—is like the sky, which is unfailingly vast, pure, and unchanging. Within this profound nature, the qualities of Buddhahood are like the rays of light that come from the sun. The inconceivable and bountiful expression of the enlightened qualities is like the ocean, in which all the stars and planets are reflected. In such a way, the Buddha's enlightened qualities are naturally present within ourselves. We simply need to actualize them, to unveil and discover them, to free our minds from delusion by means of practicing bodhicitta along the path.

The difference between the impure and the pure mind, the deluded mind and the enlightened mind, is mainly a difference of narrowness and openness. In our present deluded state, our mind is extremely narrow. For example, we live alone and rarely, if ever, consider the infinity of sentient beings. The more constricted and narrow the mind, the more it thinks only of itself, completely disregarding the well-being, happiness, and suffering of others. Conversely, the enlightened Buddha is one who considers the infinity of sentient beings, rather than being concerned with his own ego and individuality. Thus the entire path—from an ordinary being to Buddhahood—is the gradual opening of mind. And that is precisely what we call the *chang-chub* or *sem-kye*: literally, to grow and develop that enlightened attitude. The concept of "growth" is used here for the passing from a completely narrow attitude, focused principally on oneself, to an open, loving heart whose scope instinctively encompasses the infinity of sentient beings.

Starting from a totally egotistic attitude, we need to find a way to open and break through that close-fisted narrowness. How do we actually begin to be sincerely concerned with others' well-being, recognizing them as not so very different from ourselves? Basically, we can proceed like this: As a result of our being selfish, we have a natural affection and love for our parents, who gave us life and brought us up in this present life. If we utilize that spontaneous feeling that is already present, we can extend it slowly and gradually to other beings. With skillful means, we first think of our mother's kindness in giving us birth, taking care of us, educating us, and so on. From this appreciation for our mother's kindness will arise the wish to repay the mother's kindness, and the mind will begin to open to the altruistic attitude. Taking that as a basis, we can intentionally extend that basic warmth to relatives and on to other beings. This is the basis of the process of meditation to increase loving kindness to all sentient beings.

One of the first steps in meditating on bodhicitta is to become aware of the kindness of other beings. As the Buddha taught, this starts by appreciating the kindness of our own mother. For instance, if somebody gives us one hundred dollars or offers to drive us to our destination, we think he is a very kind person. But actually this is so minute compared with the kindness of our mother, who has made our body out of her own flesh and cared for us day and night while we were helpless. Once we are born, we cannot remain even ten minutes without our mother constantly taking care of us. Thus the Buddha himself said that to give the gift of the body is one of the greatest kindnesses we can find in the world. We need to become aware and appreciate that kindness. If we just think, "There is nothing to it, after all. She did that for her own benefit, her own good," that is a very serious misunderstanding. In order to develop bodhicitta, we first must become aware, and grateful, and appreciate the immense kindness of the one who gave us this existence, as well as anyone else who benefits us.

Even in the ordinary world, it is a matter of common sense that if someone has been doing a great kindness to us, and we are grateful and behave in a way to repay his kindness, everyone will think we have done the right thing. But if someone does something very good for us, and in return we treat him in a very evil way, then everyone will think we are a bad person.

We should start to appreciate others' kindness, especially our mother's. Then we should consider that throughout our many lives there is not a single being that has not been our mother or father at one time or another. Therefore, there is no reason we should not feel the same natural love and gratefulness that we have for our parents in this life, towards all sentient beings. That leads to a vast attitude, bodhicitta—to have the same gratefulness to each and every sentient being without discrimination, and to wish them all good in the same way we wish all good for our parents of this life.

Because the mind has this potential to become enlightened, through practice it can grow more and more. This is why the bodhicitta can flourish and become extremely vast. And once it has become vast, it has boundless power.

There are many examples of the power of compassion in the lives of the saints. For example, there was a famous saint named Lobpon Pawo, who meditated all the time on compassion. Once he came upon a starving tigress in the forest who was unable to feed her cubs. He thought of giving his body to the tigress. But even though he was a perfect bodhisattva, when the time came to give his body, he experienced a natural hesitation and doubt. He transformed that doubt to a complete openness to the possibility of offering his body. To describe that complete blooming of his bodhicitta, his compassion, before giving his blood to the tigress, he used his own blood to write verses on how to develop bodhicitta on the stones. These *shlokas* can still be found in the *Tengyur*. Then he gave his body to the tigers.

An eleventh century Tibetan bodhisattva, an incarnation of Shantideva named Gyalse Ngulchu Thomay—who composed the highly renowned *Thirty Seven Practices of the Bodhisattvas*—had all the animals living in peace in his hermitage. Even wolves and sheep would play together, although they are usually fierce enemies. This was because his constant meditation on bodhicitta and loving kindness was so strong that it could change the minds of even wild and fierce animals.

It is possible to truly develop bodhicitta through our practice. There was a great teacher called Nyoshul Lungtok who was one of the main disciples of Patrul Rinpoche. He began by meditating for ten years in a cave, contemplating only bodhicitta. One day Nyoshul Lungtok was just above a forest on a small hill, when he heard in the plains below a sound, like someone riding a horse and singing happy songs. Although Nyoshul Lungtok could not see him, he could hear him. Since he was such an advanced yogi, Lungtok looked into his own clairvoyant mind and saw that the horseman had only one day more to live. When he thought of the horse, he saw that the horse had only one more week to live. Suddenly he realized that the man, without thinking about it and without worries, did not realize the shortness and tenuousness of life, the imperfection of samsara, and how his karma was going to drag him from life to life into further suffering. This struck Nyoshul Lungtok so deeply that, out of sheer compassion for that man—so mindlessly happy in this ocean of suffering—he could not stop weeping for seven days. He became famous for his inconceivable spontaneous compassion and kindness towards all living things.

It is the very nature of the mind that it can be developed and evolve beyond its present limits. However, it can develop in both positive and negative ways. If we are constantly focused on negativity, the mind can grow very strong in negativity. At first it seems very difficult to kill somebody; but slowly, by becoming more cruel and inured to it, without even thinking, we could take hundreds and thousands of lives, with hardly any conflict in ourselves. Likewise, we can develop the mind in virtue.

Therefore, the main thing is to purify and train our mind, to positively transform our inner attitude and motivation. This is called *lojong* in Tibetan—mind training.

We need not think that we are only a government servant or a farmer, that we work, have a job and family, and therefore cannot be true Dharma practitioners. In one way, it is true that if we have such responsibilities and obligations we probably will not spend much of our lives absorbed in samadhi or in retreat. But in another way it is not true, because the essence of Dharma is the precious bodhicitta, which can be cultivated in any circumstances and during any activity. That is something anyone can develop in whatever occupation one may be engaged in. That is the true Dharma. Thus we can all practice the Dharma in mind, while being engaged in any form of activity with body and speech.

As it is said, "If the intention is good, then all the levels of the path will be good. If not, then all the levels will be bad." If we have a very pure heart and a clear, altruistic mind, we may encounter difficulties or sufferings, but eventually we are sure to reach bliss and happiness: it is the inevitable result of having good intention, positive attitude, and purity of heart. If we have a very wicked, disharmonious, and negative mind, we may meet with temporary success, but ultimately we will have to taste the fruit of suffering in inferior realms like the hells. It is only the quality of our minds that will result in happiness or suffering, both for ourselves and for others.

Bodhicitta can definitely be developed through intentional cultivation. To do so we can refer to various teachings, like Ngulchu Thomay's aforementioned *Thirty Seven Practices of the Bodhisattva*, or *The Seven Point Mind Training* of Atisha, or the *Bodhicaryavatara—Entering the Path of Enlightenment* by Shantideva, and other lucid teachings on transforming mind toward selfless loving kindness and compassion. This would establish an excellent basis for spiritual practice.

DEVELOPING THE RIGHT VIEW

Bodhicitta is the most essential practice of all. It simply means the excellent heart-mind that sincerely wishes to perfect itself, so that it is capable of freeing all beings from suffering. It is based on the realization that there is not one single being who does not want to be free from suffering and achieve happiness, just like ourselves. However, most beings have no way to achieve such goals. Bodhicitta has two aspects: absolute and relative, or truth and love.

In order to achieve enlightenment for the sake of all beings, we wish to receive the teachings and put them into practice. Some beings naturally have this perfect attitude and good mind, some beings have to develop it, and others have to exert great effort in getting used to the idea. But whatever the case may be, there is always a way to transform one's mind and develop bodhicitta. We can cultivate good thoughts, which lead us to nirvana, the awakened enlightenment beyond suffering; but we can also become habituated to negative thoughts, which will drag us down to the lowest states of existence. In both cases, it is by the strength of training our mind according to a certain way of thinking that leads to a particular result. That is why we must make an effort to cultivate our spiritual nature.

The Buddha explained the Dharma to sentient beings in three episodes, called "the three periods or occasions," during which the Buddha turned the wheel of the Dharma. This is also called "the three turnings of the Dharma wheel." The first was what we call the "basic teachings," including the Four Noble Truths, the Eightfold Path, the three basic characteristics of impermanence, suffering, and not-self, the twelve links comprising the chain of interdependent origination, and so on. We might mistakenly think that the Theravada or Hinayana, the so-called "Lesser Vehicle" is inferior, but this is not the case. It is best to speak of the Theravadin tradition as the Ground, Fundamental, or Root Vehicle. This means that all the teachings have to be built upon that foundation, which includes being well-grounded in the Vinaya and the sutras taught by the historical Buddha. Therefore, all the higher teachings of Mahamudra, Maha Ati or Dzogchen—the Great Perfection, and Madhyamika, must all be supported by that ground, which must be very firm and well prepared. This was the first teaching cycle of the Buddha.

THE MADHYAMIKA

Once people's minds became fit for the deeper truth, Buddha gave the second turning of the wheel of the Dharma. This deep view was the Mahayana teachings on *shunyata* and the two levels of truth—relative and absolute, and the Madhyamika or Middle Way philosophy. It is called "the turning of the wheel which is free from representations or conditioned characteristics." The teachings therein are explained according to the ground, the path, and the fruit. For the Madhyamika teachings, the *ground* is the indivisibility of the two truths: the absolute truth and the relative truth. The *path* is the indivisibility or essential union of the two accumulations: the accumulation of merits and the accumulation of wisdom. The accumulation of merit is closely connected with form and representation; the accumulation of wisdom is beyond form and representation. The *fruit* is the union or the indivisibility of the two *kayas*, the two planes or aspects of the Buddha, which are the dharmakaya, the absolute aspect of the body, and the rupakaya or form body. The rupakaya arises from the accumulation of merits and the dharmakaya from the accumulation of wisdom.

Within the Madhyamika one can distinguish two aspects: the "truth or absolute Madhyamika," and the "word Madhyamika." The former is the true nature of all things and phenomena. The word Madhyamika means the manner by which the absolute Madhyamika is expressed so that sentient beings may understand it. The absolute truth alone will not help sentient beings who are caught in ignorance to realize its ultimate meaning. Therefore, this meaning has been put into expression by enlightened beings, not through reason or discursive thought, but out of an expression of the pure wisdom that comes from enlightenment.

Word Madhyamika has two subdivisions: One is the word Madhyamika from the words of the Buddha himself. This is found in the *Prajnaparamita Sutra* and its many branches. The second is the word Madhyamika found in the commentaries written by the great followers of the Buddha, such as Nagarjuna, Chandrakirti,

Asanga, Aryadeva, and Shantideva. These elaborate on the words of the Buddha for the sake of the understanding of beings.

There are so many philosophical treatises—unless we go into all of these studies in exhaustive detail, it is difficult to get a clear idea of all the differences. Basically, in the Madhyamika the most absolute view is the Prasangika outlook upheld by Nagarjuna, Chandrakirti, and their followers. Then there is also the Svatantrika outlook within the Middle Way school.

In truth, the basic ground and the true nature of everything is shunyata, great emptiness. This is the same in all the Madhyamika schools. The only difference is in a person's capability to understand this absolute truth, this empty nature. Some see it in a narrow way, others in a completely open way. When one tries to express and think about this empty nature or shunyata, it will be expressed and expounded in different ways according to one's level and faculties. This results in the different expressions of the absolute view, although the basic ground is always the empty nature itself, which is adamantine, forever unchanging, and beyond all these various kinds of teachings.

The basic subject of the Madhyamika is the two truths, absolute and relative. The word *Uma*, which refers in Tibetan to Madhyamika, really means "center" or "middle." It refers to the absolute truth. Why do we call it middle? Because it does not fall into any extreme, and remains always in the center. Basically, we can conceive of four extremes: existent, non-existent, origination, and cessation. For the proper view of the absolute truth, one must not believe in any of these extremes; one must remain in a state that neither exists nor does not exist, without origination nor cessation, beyond both and neither as well.

We can also speak of these concepts as extremes: coming and going, having an origin and a cessation, existing and non-existing, identical and different, and so on. The basic view of the Madhyamika is the view of emptiness that is beyond all such extremes. It is called the view of the *dharmata* or absolute nature, which is likened to the sky: without boundaries, without center and periphery, inside and outside; beyond conditions and limitations. The absolute truth is beyond any reference point or qualification.

When we speak of the relative truth, it refers to the whole phenomenal world, the different aspects of life: the universe and sentient beings, how they seem to appear, their characteristics, the different elements, aggregates, consciousnesses, and so on. The explanation of the way in which manifestations arise and develop—though never parting from the empty nature of the absolute truth—is what we call the relative truth, and implies the operation of the law of karma. The main point is to realize that the two truths are not separate. The true nature of the phenomenal world is emptiness, and within that emptiness the phenomenal world appears.

The basic teachings of these two truths were explained by Nagarjuna in five main treatises of the Madhyamika. They were further elaborated by Aryadeva in the treatise called the *Four Hundred Stanzas*. The *panditas* of India and Tibet, such as Longchenpa and Tsongkhapa, continued to build a vast spectrum of literature upon the Madhyamika, but it all comes down to understanding the two truths and their relation to one another.

When we say that all phenomena are empty, it does not mean a mere blank or sterile vacuum, devoid of the slightest quality or potential. It is, in fact, something that bears great qualities and great potential for awakened enlightenment.

For instance, if we say, "This cup is empty," there is no great quality in that recognition. Or if we say, "That space is empty," it is like finding something which does not help much. But recognizing that all phenomena are empty through the Madhyamika view bears much fruit and great possible achievements. Someone who realizes that all phenomena are empty, and realizes the nonexistence of self or ego, will naturally have spontaneous, effortless compassion for all sentient beings who do not realize the truth of emptiness, and who continue to suffer through delusion and clinging. To recognize and progress in our realization of the empty, open, selfless nature, is what will bring us to full enlightenment, and unfold all the other boundless qualities of spiritual realization. It will produce the pure perception where we can perceive the buddha-nature in every being.

For ordinary beings who are in mental darkness, ignorance, and delusion, to simply present the fact that everything is empty will not help them to get rid of that delusion: just as in a dream, there is nothing actually happening, yet while you are dreaming you perceive it as a fact, as your condition, and react accordingly. Because beings actually experience delusion as if it were something truly existent, they need to rely on the methods of relative truth. It is necessary to bring them to a gradual understanding of the absolute truth. If there were no delusion, there wouldn't be a need for all these teachings about the relative truth. But as long as sentient beings remain caught in ignorance, they need to rely upon these teachings; they need to rely upon the laws that occur within the unfolding of relative truth: that is, the law of all phenomena, the ineluctable karmic law of cause and effect.

That understanding of emptiness is reached by the understanding of true selflessness, which means the nonexistence of the separate, individual self, and the nonexistence of independent phenomena. All dharmas—outer phenomena and mental events or *noumena*—are actually lacking in independent existence.

The nonexistence of the individual self has been clearly expounded by Chandrakirti in a seven-fold analysis. He uses an example of a chariot as being like the so-called individual *atman*, which is only an agglomeration of elements with interdependent factors, and has little or nothing to do with what we call the self of an individual. The chariot is not the wheel, not the axles. We cannot even find an entity by putting these things together. It is purely a label put on something and does not exist by itself: like naming a group of stars the "Big Dipper," when there is no dipper anywhere to be found or to be used to pour liquids. Having understood the nonexistence of the individual self, one will come to analyze the nonexistence of phenomena in general. Then one will easily understand the meaning of the inseparability of the two truths: the empty, open nature, and the unceasing magical appearance of all phenomena.

The ground of the Madhyamika is the two truths: the absolute and the relative. The path of the Madhyamika is the way to directly experience the truth of the union of the relative and the absolute. This is done through the accumulation of merit and wisdom. Accumulation of wisdom means to remain in a state of equanimity, and in the contemplation of emptiness—shunyata—which is beyond all concepts and characteristics. Remaining evenly in that absolute nature is what we mean by meditation. When there is accumulation of merit during the post-meditation period, it is because our way of acting is connected with the understanding of the void nature, and therefore it naturally turns towards virtue.

The accumulation of wisdom is beyond any representation; the accumulation of merits is associated with representation. When we think of the six perfections or *paramitas*—generosity, ethical discipline, patience, diligence, meditative concentration, and wisdom—there will be a thought of helping others. Hence, there is a subject, object, and action, and a type of conceptual framework or representation. The path of the Madhyamika combines the understanding of absolute emptiness in meditation with the application of such understanding in impeccable bodhisattva activity, thus fulfilling the accumulation of merits through the six paramitas and ultimately actualizing Buddhahood.

The reason to accomplish these two accumulations is not for their own sake; rather, it is because there is a fruit that issues from these accumulations. The fruit of the accumulation of wisdom is the dharmakaya; the fruit of the accumulation of merit is the rupakaya. The dharmakaya is the ultimate goal of the realization of the absolute nature or dharmata, the empty nature of all phenomena, the union of emptiness and appearances. This realization has boundless enlightened qualities which spontaneously manifest just like rays emanating from the sun. We speak of the Buddha's ten strengths, the eighteen absences of confusion, the ten powers, and so on—these are all the enlightened qualities of a fully enlightened Buddha, and are inherent in the dharmakaya or absolute body. That itself is the buddha-nature and the fruit of the accumulation of wisdom. This means that the Buddhas will spontaneously emanate manifestations, such as spiritual teachers, bodhisattvas, and so forth, in order to help sentient beings in countless ways.

Within the rupakaya or form body, we distinguish between the sambhogakaya—manifestation at the subtle level, and the nirmanakaya—manifestation at the gross level. The latter is what ordinary beings can perceive. The nirmanakaya includes manifestations such as *tulkus*—reincarnate bodhisattva-lamas, spiritual teachers, great bodhisattvas, and incarnate Buddhas like Buddha Shakyamuni. The three jewels can also manifest as anything beneficial to beings, such as medicine, bridges, scriptures, statues, and so forth. In this way, the fruit of the two accumulations is both the absolute realization of enlightenment (*dharmakaya*), and all its numerous manifestations for the sake of sentient beings (*rupakaya*).

It is very easy to say that the nature of everything is emptiness, and emptiness is inseparable from forms and appearances. However this is an extremely deep and difficult idea to thoroughly comprehend. The great Madhyamika is a subject as vast as enlightenment itself. Compared with the view of Madhyamika, what we ordinarily perceive is like the difference between what we see through a hole in a needle or a drinking straw, and directly seeing the sky itself. When we say "emptiness," it is the same emptiness, whether narrowly or broadly viewed, as in the straw's-eye-view analogy, but there is a great difference in magnitude, understanding, and actual realization. It requires more than mere intellectual understanding. A true understanding of emptiness grows deeper, ever more and more expansive, towards the realization of the fundamental union of the absolute truth of emptiness and the relative truth of the karmic law of phenomena—it grows into the complete realization of enlightenment.

Throughout our practice, we need to constantly make our mind broader, less rigid, and more open. This effort is worthwhile in so many ways. In our ordinary activities, our mind is often narrow and closed in upon itself; it is very difficult to achieve any goal, to really relate and have an unselfish attitude towards others. Such close-mindedness can only lead to miserable consequences. On the other hand, if we diligently try to open our minds, we will naturally have compassion, faith in the three jewels, inner peace, and a pure perception of others. This attitude will not only lead to a happy life free from obstacles, but it is precisely the way to gradually understand the absolute truth and the profound nature of everything just as it is, in a completely open and unconditioned way. In both our meditation and the activities of daily life, it is very important for us to continually open our mind and free it from its limitations, gradually transcending concepts, mental darkness, conflicting emotions, and delusion.

One can see in the life of exalted beings how powerful is the realization of truth. The realization of emptiness naturally provides boundless compassion and pure perception. The ultimate point of the absolute truth is the realization of emptiness. The ultimate practice of the relative truth is the practice of bodhicitta, compassion.

When we speak of the indivisibility of the two truths, it is because when one realizes emptiness, one will naturally and spontaneously have compassion; there will be no need to fabricate it. Practicing bodhicitta will automatically lead us to the understanding of the absolute truth. These are not two distinct things; rather, they always appear together. This is why it is important to constantly associate them—trying to develop our understanding of the absolute truth while trying to use the skillful means of bodhicitta. Our practice of the two truths, relative and absolute, must go together inseparably. We must understand from above with the absolute outlook, while practicing climbing up the spiritual mountain from below with relative practices, according to our individual capacity and inclination. That is what is meant in the Dzogchen teachings by the phrase, "swooping down from above while climbing up from below," the practice combining the two levels of truth, also known as "understanding according to the supreme view and practicing according to ones ability." This is the most complete and efficacious form of spiritual practice, which can be applied in the context of almost any particular form of practice—including the ordinary activities of daily life.

These are just a few words of teaching. What we need for this or any other teaching is to constantly train our hearts and minds in order to open, unfold, gentle, and transform them. First, listen to the teachings, then ponder deeply upon them, and finally assimilate them, through applying them into actual practice. If we do so, it is just like the alchemical transformation of base metal into gold. When we perform the alchemical process, if we begin with iron, it will be transformed into gold; if it is copper, it will be transformed into gold; if it is silver, it will be transformed into gold. Similarly, if we apply this mind-training practice with bodhicitta, whether we are involved in worldly activities, working for ourselves or for others, for the government, in business, and so forth, we will transform all such activities into the path of the Dharma. Just as alchemy turns any metal into gold, bodhicitta practice will turn any activity, any thought, anything we say, into a Dharma practice. So it is extremely important to maintain, continue, and increase mind training.

Why do we make a prayer of dedication and sharing the merits at the end of the teaching? It is because the efficacy of anything positive we do depends upon whether or not we dedicate it. If we dedicate a positive action for the benefit of all beings with the wish that they may achieve enlightenment, it will truly help all beings to attain that state, for we are all connected and interdependent. Prayers are very powerful, effective, and far-reaching. The energy of that positive action will then continue ceaselessly, from the very moment of dedication until the goal is reached.

If we do not dedicate the merit to all sentient beings, the positive energy can immediately vanish. In the very moment of a virtuous act, it will have a positive effect, but it will not carry forward, nor will it greatly help us and others to reach enlightenment. It is always best to dedicate the action while remaining in the understanding of the absolute nature, just like the understanding of all the perfect Buddhas. Saying hundreds of such dedication prayers would infinitely benefit our progress and help bring other beings to enlightenment. Therefore the dedications are very deep, profound, and important. These should never be neglected, but should always be applied to any practice as well as any good action done in our daily lives.

3   You Are Dzogpa Chenpo
*A Teaching On Relative and Absolute Bodhicitta
at a Two-Month Dzogchen Retreat in America*

All the enlightened ones have realized perfect supreme buddhahood; all beings, including ourselves, can also do so. It is not just something private between lamas and their students. It is something that unfolds the infinity of our own original nature, our innermost heart and mind, bodhicitta, a gift inseparable from all living things.

On the relative level of everyday life, bodhicitta is compassion, loving-kindness, and unconditional acceptance. On the ultimate or absolute level, bodhicitta includes the most empty, void, open, mysterious aspects of being. These are the two sides of bodhicitta: relative and absolute, truth and love.

Whatever we do with selfish, narrow, egotistical motivation is very limited and probably temporary. When we act with concern only for this lifetime, in this *saha* (thorny, rosebush-like) world, our scope is contracted from what it could be. There is a Tibetan saying that "everything rests on the tip of one's motivation." This indicates the significance in every moment, of cultivating altruistic, selfless intention—bodhicitta. Endowed with such a luminous heart, even the smallest words, deeds, and actions that one accomplishes have vast and beneficial implications. This is the transforming magic of bodhicitta, a veritable wish-fulfilling jewel, not unlike the proverbial philosophers' stone that turns whatever it touches to gold.

With the profoundly significant and meaningful altruistic bodhicitta, whether we perform large or small actions, there are vast and far-reaching benefits for beings everywhere—including beings of the past, present, and future—since the scope of the motivation explicitly includes all beings. Whether the activity is meditation, prayer, or another explicit spiritual practice, whatever we do depends upon our motivation.

According to the karmic law of cause and effect, the fruit infallibly follows the seed or cause, which is primarily our motivation, and secondarily depends on our physical actions. When we work just for our own pleasure or happiness, to feed ourselves, or to find comfort for ourselves, this is what is called a small mind or narrow outlook. It is not even like working for our family or our parents, or as a guardian for our children. When we open that motivation up a little bit towards our family and friends, the heart and mind opens somewhat. The most important thing is to have a good heart, a pure and sincere heart, which is actually the fundamental essence of us all, even if we don't usually actualize it.

Often we find ourselves involved in strife with family, colleagues, and so forth. It is important and helpful to recognize that this may inevitably arise, yet it does not need to be seen as a big problem. For everything depends on our intention. We can work with anything and integrate it into the path, our spiritual practice, through pure mind and good heart, always from the point of view of benefiting others. The very heart-essence of Buddhadharma is to benefit others, bodhicitta. Whatever else we might do is secondary to that. And if we cultivate this good heart, this altruistic unselfish attitude, then all strife and struggle will naturally be pacified, purified, transformed, and even become beneficial to others, through contact with that good heart, which we—the bodhisattvas—strive to embody.

Even if we study spirituality for years, if we have a mixed, impure motivation, a selfish attitude, our path is limited and our development is restricted. If a teacher gives excellent discourses and other forms of teachings but his motivation is mixed, the benefit of those teachings is also extremely limited. A spiritual teacher also has to impeccably embody purity of heart, being suffused with the spontaneous generosity and warmth of service-oriented, altruistic bodhicitta: bodhi-mind—the sterling aspiration to be able to truly help others and relieve misery, in both the relative and ultimate sense.

People commonly find themselves in difficult relationships. As long as we are still subject to karma and *klesha*—conflicting emotions—there will inevitably be countless ups and downs. Yet, if people are committed to helping each other, to serving each other, to growing and awakening together, then all circumstances and situations are perfectly workable, whatever roller-coaster-like dips and turns unexpectedly come along. This is an example of practicing bodhicitta by actually applying it in our daily life, which is actually the principal point.

When we practice bodhicitta prayers or meditations, it may look like we are alone, like we are practicing for ourselves, but we are not practicing for ourselves, and we are not alone. All beings are interconnected, and in that sense they are present or affected. Milarepa sang, "When I am alone, meditating in the mountains, all the Buddhas past, present, and future are with me. Guru Marpa is always with me. All beings are here."

We are not practicing for ourselves alone, since everybody is involved and included in the great scope of our prayers and meditations on this perfectly pure motivation. The natural outflow of so-called "solitary meditation or prayer" is spontaneous benefit for others; it's like the rays of the sun, rays which spontaneously reach out. This good heart, pure heart, vast and open mind, is called in Tibetan *sem karpo*, white mind. It means pure, vast, and open heart. This is innate bodhicitta. It is not something foreign to us, as we well know, yet it is something we could relate to more, cultivate, generate, and embody. We talk about vast and profound teachings of Dharma, such as Dzogchen, but without this goodness of heart, this unselfishness, it is mere chatter, gossip, and rationalization.

If a man is looking for a companion, sometimes he is only thinking that he wants a woman to make him happy for his own reasons. Not often is he thinking how he can benefit or help his companion. Such a relationship is already built on the tip of a very limited motivation or intention, and the results of that are questionable. Many people stay in a hotel; the hotel is very interested in making the guests happy, but in general their sole motivation is business. The reason to make the guests happy is for their own profit. What ultimate benefit can there be in trying to make people happy in such a limited way, simply for one's own profit?

If one practices the incredibly rare and profound teaching of Dzogchen, nondual Dzogchen, with an intention like this: "I want Dzogchen, I want enlightenment. I'm going to get it in this life," and there is a great deal of grasping, pushy, small-minded selfishness, how can there be any Dzogchen? This is the very antithesis of the vast, unconditional openness of Dzogchen. This is how we stray from the true path and become wild practitioners and even become crazy. If self-clinging, self-cherishing, and clinging to the reality of things remains strong, how can there be any genuine Dzogchen, which is the true natural state of freedom, openness, and primordial perfection?

If you practice bodhicitta practices—mind training, loving-kindness prayers, exchanging oneself and others (*tong len*), and so forth—these practices may seem conceptual and relative, but they actually include the absolute truth that is the very nature of Dzogchen: vast openness, big mind, purity, freedom, and nongrasping. Unselfishness is no different than that nondual openness, vast emptiness, *shunyata*. Dzogchen may be as primordially pure and ever unaffected as the virgin snow, but approaching it with mixed motivation or impure selfish aspiration is a great limitation. When you urinate in the snow, the snow starts white, but suddenly it's yellow.

The word for bodhicitta in Tibetan is *sem kye*. This literally means "the opening or blossoming of the mind." It is the opposite of small mind, of self-preoccupation, self-contraction, and narrowness. Whatever practice-path we find ourselves on—be it Dzogchen, Vajrayana, the Bodhisattvayana, the fundamental Theravadin Vehicle, or another spiritual path—if we have a pure, wholesome attitude and a spacious and tolerant mind, then our practice is really Buddhist practice; it is in line with practice that really blossoms and unties the mind. This is the real meaning of bodhicitta.

It may be that the sky is always limpid, clear, vast, infinite, and so on, but when the moment of Dzogchen arrives it is as if the sun has suddenly risen. It is not that the sky of our inherent nature has improved, but something definitely does seem to happen. This metaphor of the rising sun refers to the *rangjung yeshe*, the spontaneous, self-born awareness wisdom or innate wakefulness dawning within our nature. This is the moment of Dzogchen, the dawn of the self-arisen awareness wisdom, innate wisdom.

This is the meaning of what is called in Tibetan *nyur de dzogpa chenpo*, meaning "swift and comfy innate Great Perfection"—a path that does not require austerities or arduous practices. It is direct, swift, spacious, natural, and comfy. It is doable!

In one lifetime, in one body, even in one instant of self-arisen awareness, this dawn of Vajrasattva—the self-born innate awareness wisdom—shines forth like a blazing inner sun. When you relate to this self-arisen innate awareness wisdom, when you practice Dzogchen as it actually is, this fleeting human existence is instantaneously made meaningful. And not just this life, but all our lives are made meaningful, as well as the lives of all those who have been connected with us. This experience of the natural state of the luminous innate Great Perfection implies the annihilation, the crashing into dust, of all forms of self-clinging and duality, of clinging to the concrete reality of things, to their appearances.

The inherent freedom of being is spontaneously, primordially present. All delusory perceptions are naturally nonexistent in this dawn of innate awareness wisdom. The proliferation of karma and klesha is based on dualistic clinging, ignorance: in the light of nondual awareness, the kleshas do not obtain. Everything "falls apart" because it is inherently unborn from the beginning; and the freedom of perfect being, of *rigpa*, spontaneously present since the beginningless beginning, is clearly and thoroughly realized in that very moment.

It is easy to stray into sidetracks in this vast, luminous profundity. Of course we know that we need a vast, open, altruistic bodhimind. We can see that the innate Great Perfection, the ultimate nature of things, is beyond the conceptual mind and its dualistic perceptions. But still—here the deviation point comes in—still we are spying, searching in a very constricted and pointed way, wondering: What is Dzogchen? Where is Dzogchen? What is it? I want to perceive and experience it.

This is natural, but it precedes the recognition of our true nature. This is a deviation point that, after recognition, is not necessary to indulge in. It is like after meeting and getting to know someone, one doesn't have to think too much to imagine what that person looks like or is like: there is an intuitive freedom from such doubts and speculations, and one gets on with more direct, first-hand appreciation.

We can make many productive inquiries, such as, when a thought arises, noticing: That's a thought. Where does it arise from? Where is it going? Where did it go? Where is the gap or open space between thoughts that I heard about in Mahamudra teachings, which I'm supposed to recognize?

This has little to do with actual Dzogchen practice: this is mind practice, mind-made meditation, not rigpa practice *per se*. Yet these questions are part of the explicit preliminaries to Dzogchen practice and help one to distinguish between mind (*sems*) and innate wakefulness (*rigpa*).

The danger is that we hear too much too soon. We think we have understood shunyata, err on the side of the absolute in a nihilistic fashion, and are obscured by concepts. Nagarjuna said, "It is sad to see those who mistakenly believe in material, concrete reality, but far more pitiful are those who believe in emptiness." Those who believe in things can be helped through various kinds of practice, through the way of skillful means, but those who have fallen into the abyss of emptiness find it almost impossible to re-emerge, since there seem to be no handholds, no steps, no gradual progression, and nothing to do.

One easily becomes ensnared by the tangled undergrowth of ideas. Then we exhaust ourselves in fruitless speculation, become disillusioned, and eventually give up. This is the danger with hearing nondual teachings, such as Dzogchen and shunyata, before one has actually experienced and practiced them. But who is the one that's making these questionable, somewhat fallacious efforts? It's the discursive or conceptual mind, the *namtok*-er. *Namtok* means conceptuality, discursive thinking; it refers to the dualistic mind. The namtok-er means the namtok-mind, the dualistic conceptual mind that produces inexhaustibly all these questionable efforts.

The namtok machine, the divisive intellect, has two kinds of families. One family is the group of the three poisons (*kleshas*), or the five poisons, which represent the entire proliferation of the eighty-four thousand kleshas traditionally mentioned; these include all the different varieties of thoughts, negative and positive emotions, delusions, and so on. This namtok-er, the dualistic mind, has three departments: past thoughts, present thoughts, and future thoughts.

This namtok machine, this dualistic mind, also has three groups of in-laws or relatives: virtuous thoughts, words, and deeds; nonvirtuous thoughts, words, and deeds; and neutral thoughts, words, and deeds. It is not just a question of the negative emotions—such as hatred, delusion, and attachment—being namtok. Even virtuous thoughts, acts, and deeds—like love, compassion, and devotion—are namtok. The neutral or indifferent—and even subconscious, unacknowledged thoughts—are also namtok, for they are within the reality of finite mind, duality, and ignorance.

How, then, to relate to all these families and tribes of namtok? How to live the truth of Dharma in daily life, where it really counts, where it can actually make a difference? By practicing the truth of simultaneously self-arising and self-liberating intrinsic awareness. Everything in our experience is actually spontaneously appearing, spontaneously changing, spontaneously liberating or releasing, without our help. We don't need to interfere, to manipulate, to fabricate anything. That's the Dzogchen outlook on how to relate to everything, both in formal meditation sessions and in post-meditation, in everyday life. It combines all three aspects of rigpa practice: view, meditation, and action.

Dzogchen, the natural Great Perfection, is supposed to be a practice and view, an outlook or perspective, beyond the conceptual mind. Therefore, being involved either for or against phenomenal appearances—that is, circumstantial conditions, whether inner or outer, either indulging or suppressing namtok—is mind-made meditation. This is fabrication and contrivance, not rigpa practice. It is like a dog chasing its tail. It is not Dzogchen practice, the liberating natural nonpractice of spontaneous arising and spontaneous release.

Until one recognizes the insubstantial, empty, dream-like nature of all namtok, all forms and appearances, all states of mind, including both mental *noumena* and external phenomena, and one recognizes their open luminous nature, including one's own selfless, open, and luminous primordial buddha-nature; until one is free from fixation, willful involvement, or compulsive reactivity;

karma is inevitably accumulated. However, in abiding by rigpa—recognizing one's original nature, enjoying the natural flow of innate wakefulness, nondual intrinsic awareness—the very root of karmic cause and effect, of suffering, is severed. Moreover, the conditions that ripen latent karmic seeds can no longer come together, so even the karmic residue of past actions finds no place to ripen. It is like the arising of the waves in the ocean: they do not improve, ruin, disturb, or really even change the ocean in any way, except perhaps on the most superficial level.

This is how we can, in the way of Dzogchen, relate to our own buddha-nature: through and amidst all appearances, all arisings, all circumstances and conditions, integrating every activity into the spiritual journey. This reveals the innate freedom and perfection of Dzogchen, the immutable or unchanging ocean-like nature of awareness itself.

If we are chained by hope and fear, expectation and anxiety, we again need to reorient ourselves, use the view of Dzogchen as a pole star in order to better navigate. For it is a sign that we are not abiding in rigpa, but are still involved with mere conceptual mind, which is not Dzogchen practice.

However, how can we cut off our search before it has been totally fulfilled? We need to recognize the nature of the searcher in order for our search to be fulfilled.

Devotion and trust in our teacher is the one practice that can assure that we stay close to the essence of the Dzogchen path. Some people prematurely conclude that such an essentialized, direct, and naked teaching as the nondual Great Perfection teachings of Dzogchen does not, and even should not, require faith, devotion, or relative practice, or, for that matter, any kind of intentional cultivation at all. Such people jump to the hasty conclusion that the altruistic bodhicitta, virtuous activities, morality and related spiritual practices have nothing to do with the natural practice of the profound Great Perfection.

From one point of view one can say this is true, or perhaps that it is close to the truth. It is true that all these things are within the context of relative truth, the dimension of mind (*sems*). This is undeniable. Such spiritual efforts are not necessarily identical with Dzogchen itself, which is the absolute reality beyond the mind.

Therefore it is not inaccurate to, at some point, think that faith, devotion, purposeful effort, and the cultivation of relative practices are not Dzogchen itself—the absolute nature of things, the absolute truth, the self-arisen or the spontaneous innate awareness wisdom. It is true that these relative practices are mind, are namtok; that they are not Dzogchen itself.

However, these relative practices are very, very important for those who, like ourselves, are still involved in living in the relative world. We cannot deny the operation of karma and how our conditioning continues to bind us. For someone who instantaneously realizes, and in the same instant totally actualizes, the perfect buddhahood of Dzogchen—which is none other than rigpa— they would no longer have to do anything relative: they would no longer be in this world. Yet as long as they were embodied and walking this earth, they would probably be decent, sane human beings....Why harm others, who are just like ourselves?

If you want to enter a house you need to go through a door. Of course it is true that, in the beginning, you need to go through a door, but after you understand about houses you see other ways to enter, such as windows, down the chimney, and so forth. But we will probably still use the door in most cases, although we are not necessarily limited to that manner of entry or approach. Similarly, having actualized rigpa, absolute truth, one usually continues to function within relative reality, manifesting in a sane and ordinary fashion, living ethically, acting compassionately, and so on. Why wouldn't we? H.H. Khyentse Rinpoche said, "When you truly understand the absolute truth of shunyata, emptiness, you understand the relative truth level workings of karma. What else puts anything into motion?"

Dzogchen is like the key to the sky, an open space that includes the space within the house: faith, trust, and devotion are like the key to the door. The space within and without the house are both like the vast, accommodating expanse of rigpa itself, but to enter at first, it seems that one needs a key. Moreover, it seems to most of us that we usually need to live inside a house, although actually that is just a concept someone came up with sometime after the era of the ape-men. Do you see how we cannot deny the expediency of conceptual frameworks, even if they are somewhat limited?

In this analogy, the key seems different from the house; but to enter a locked house, one needs a key. Faith and devotion are like the key to that house, the spacious mansion of the innate Great Perfection. Once one is actually in the house, one knows what the house is and can enjoy it in different ways.

Precious bodhicitta, the invaluable trust, devotion, compassion, and all the relative practices are extraordinarily helpful and supportive for the absolute realization called Dzogchen; all the Vajramasters concur on this crucial point. All these aspects of the relative and absolute levels of reality are actually inseparably connected. The ultimate realization, or absolute aspect of bodhicitta, is Dzogchen, rigpa, *tathagatagarbha* or buddha-nature. This is the great mansion, the ultimate abode we are talking about.

In the beginning one might conceive of keys and doors, windows, ceilings, and walls, and so on. But after one has established residence inside, it's like the fabled island of jewels, which is like the experience of this primordial innate rigpa. Even if one searches on that fabulous island, one cannot find the smallest ordinary stone, pebble, or clod of dirt. Similarly, in the vast expanse of rigpa, all thoughts and feelings are simply seen as display of *dharmakaya*. One cannot find even the smallest dualistic thought or perception.

The inconceivable mansion or citadel of rigpa is like a huge, empty house. It doesn't need to be locked, protected, fortified, or maintained, for the thief-like dualistic thoughts have nothing to steal. Namtok can come and go as it will, for there is nothing there to hold onto, nothing to lose, nothing to protect. Far out! *Emaho!* What a wonder!

Everything is the nature of Dzogpa Chenpo. You are Dzogpa Chenpo, your abode is Dzogpa Chenpo, your nature is Dzogpa Chenpo—innate Great Perfection. There is nothing to gain or lose. This is the nature or state of primordial buddhahood, Kuntuzangpo (in Sanskrit, Samantabhadra), which literally means All-Good. Everything is okay, everything is fine, what needed to be done has been done.

The enlightened Dzogchen lineage holder and patriarch, Longchenpa, who was the primordial Buddha Samantabhadra in human form, explained that there are five great perfections within the luminous Great Perfection. He said that samsara is primordially perfect Samantabhadra; nirvana is primordially perfect

Samantabhadra; all perceptions and phenomenal appearances are primordially perfect Samantabhadra; emptiness itself is primordially perfect Samantabhadra; and everything is the primordial Buddha Samantabhadra. Emaho! Wonderful! That is why Samantabhadra burst forth with his famous twelve vajra laughs—cosmic laughter, an explosion of pure joy.

Saraha, too, sang such a song, dancing wildly and waving his arms, explaining that everything is "That." Saraha sang, "In the ten directions, wherever I look, there is nothing besides this primordial Buddha, which has no arms and no legs, is just one infinite, luminous sphere."

In the same song, Saraha sang, "Now that our work is completely finished, we have nothing to do and time to do whatever we want." That's the ultimate dance and song that we ourselves need to sing. When spiritual practice is authentic, that can be your song, your dance, and your reality—our reality.   What one needs is what we've already received, which can fit into the palm of our hand. Please cherish it, keep it exactly where it is right now. It is with you, whatever you aspire towards, want, and need; it is with us, and is us. However many thousands of commentaries, scriptures, and teachings may fill the airwaves with sound vibrations, the essence of them all is the recognition of the true nature of one's mind, and the practice or actualization of that.

The Christians have a big good book called the Bible, and within the Bible there are two different Bibles, and moreover there are libraries full of commentaries since the time when the Bible first arose. Those two Bibles exist in Tibetan in an outdated nineteenth century translation by some Jesuit missionaries. In Hinduism there are the Vedas, Upanishads, the *Bhagavad Gita* and so on. So many splendid scriptures and commentaries, many of which have been translated very well into Tibetan over the last thousand years. The Koran also has quite a few pages, and plenty of other writings over the last thousand years are derived from that source. And outside the religious and spiritual traditions of the world there are so many books, philosophies, sciences, psychology, political notions, and other interesting things to read and study and think about, just like the infinite leaves in a wild forest.

But whether one knows all those things or not, if and when one discovers and recognizes spontaneous innate awareness wisdom, the true nature of all things—called Dzogpa Chenpo or innate buddha-nature—that is the heart of the matter, which is all one needs. That is the universal panacea, which cures all ills, resolves all delusions and doubts, and which totally liberates and frees.

The seventeen Dzogchen tantras are like scriptures of the primordial Buddha. The main one is called the *Kunshi Gyalpo Gyu, The Tantra of the Sovereign of all Activities.* If one understands the meaning of Dzogchen, just hearing the title of such a tantra explains everything: that there is just one great sovereign, the master of all activities—referring, of course, to rigpa or buddha-nature, one's own original nature. The only import of practice is to understand, recognize, and truly experience deeply the true nature of all things.

If you really want to study and hear about Dzogchen, there are many writings: there is the famous enlightened trilogy by Longchenpa, translated by Guenther as *The Trilogy of Comfort and Ease*, and his other profound trilogy, the *Rangdrol Korsum*, as yet untranslated; the *Seven Treasures* by Longchenpa; many vajra-songs by Rigdzin Jigme Lingpa, including his exhaustive *Yonten Dzod*; and many delightful writings by the enlightened turn-of-the-century vagabond, Patrul Rinpoche, and his contemporary, Lama Mipham. More recently, the late great Nyingma leader, H.H. Dudjom Rinpoche, our beloved master, adorned this world with his numerous enlightened poems, writings, and treasure-texts. There's a whole universe of such things; we are very fortunate to be connected to them.

We are also fortunate in that we don't have to read them all. Scriptures, teachings, and practices are not the ultimate way, they are reflections of it. The true meaning of Dzogchen is your own nature, not something you need to find outside. Truth is not really found in books, it is only described in books. It is not like food, which must be eaten and comes from outside. Dharma teachings are not exactly like food, which can only temporarily satisfy hunger; realizing the ultimate nature of reality within is the only truly long-lasting fulfillment and utmost satisfaction.

Dzogchen itself is the three jewels. It is our own original nature of body, speech, and mind: the three *kayas* or buddha-bodies. Let that rest in natural great ease, carefree ease, at home and at peace with all things. There's no need to focus one-pointedly on any object, or to analyze and try to figure out and understand things. Those are preliminary bases for beginners, in the light of this sort of absolute, nondual practice. Once you have been introduced to your true nature, and have recognized it, you can really begin to practice Dzogchen. Therefore, remain in the innate great ease, open to everything, aware of innate wakefulness itself, the natural state.

One of the best books by the omniscient Longchenpa is *Semnyi Ngalso, The Natural Ease of Mind.* This refers to innate ease, not the end-product of incredible efforts and striving. *Semnyi Ngalso* is also the name applied to his particular meditation posture, with hands on knees and straightforward, natural gaze. If you want to study all of Longchenpa's writings, rest in the innate great ease of this *asana*: this would complete your study.

Enjoy the innate Great Perfection, it's all yours.

4 Ground, Path, and Fruition

*Mind-Nature Teachings Concerning the View,
Meditation, and Action of Dzogpa Chenpo, the
Innate Great Perfection*

Compiled by Surya Das with Nyoshul Khenpo

*Homage to the primordial Buddha Samantabhadra, the
    Buddha within!*
Homage to the omniscient master Gyalwa Longchenpa!

Buddha-nature, the essence of awakened enlightenment itself, is present in everyone. Its essence is forever pure, unalloyed, and flawless. It is beyond increase or decrease. It is neither improved by remaining in nirvana nor degenerated by straying into samsara. Its fundamental essence is forever perfect, unobscured, quiescent, and unchanging. Its expressions are myriad.

Those who recognize their true nature are enlightened; those who ignore or overlook it are deluded. There is no way to enlightenment other than by recognizing buddha-nature and achieving stability in that, which implies authentically identifying it within one's own stream of being, and training in that incisive recognition through simply sustaining its continuity, without alteration or fabrication.

All spiritual practices and paths converge, and are included, in this vital point. This recognition is the sole borderline between Buddhas and ordinary beings. This is also the great crossroads at which we find ourselves every moment of our lives. The illusory history of samsara and nirvana begins here and now; the moment of Dzogchen, the innate Great Perfection, is actually beyond past, present, and future—like a seemingly eternal instant of timeless time. This is what we call "the fourth time": timeless time, beyond the three times, the ineffable instant of pure ecstatic presence or total awareness, *rigpa.*

Rigpa—primordial being, innate awareness—is primordially awakened: free, untrammeled, perfect, and unchanging. Yet we need to recognize it within our very own being if it is to be truly realized. Rigpa is our share or portion of the *dharmakaya.* Those who overlook it have forgotten their true original nature. Subject to suffering, karma, and confusion, we must recognize rigpa in order to actualize our own total potential, the sublime joy, peace, and freedom of enlightenment itself.

The late Dilgo Khyentse Rinpoche said that the great yogis and enlightened adepts wanted and needed nothing more than the re-alization of the fundamental nature of intrinsic awareness itself. Padampa Sangye, the medieval Indian siddha who brought the Prajnaparamita Shijay and Chöd teachings to Tibet, said that all wishes and aspirations can be fulfilled within the natural state. *Emaho!* Don't overlook this.

The primordial Buddha Samantabhadra, the personification of rigpa, who is the formless dharmakaya Buddha at the source of the Dzogchen teachings and lineage, never strayed into dualistic thinking, and remains free and perfect in the infinite display of pure appearances that is his pure land or buddha-field, embracing the inseparability of everything within both samsara and nirvana.

However, deceived by deluded thoughts and appearances, sentient beings fall into dualistic thought and cling to the illusion of subject and object, thus being led into the roiling ocean of impure appearances, conditioned existence. Mistakenly perceiving the in-expressible, self-existing, innate wakefulness of primordial aware-ness for a fixed self or soul—our own egoic, individual existence—we enmesh and bind ourselves time after time, time without end.

Ignorance is the sole cause of wandering in samsara. Buddhas know and understand what ordinary sentient beings ignore, misunderstand, and overlook: the true original nature of one and all. That is the sole distinction between Buddhas and ordinary beings.

Tulku Urgyen Rinpoche said, "The confusion that arose in...the path can be cleared away. When we remove the temporary stains from primordially awakened rigpa, we become re-enlightened instead of primordially enlightened. This is accomplished by following the oral instructions of a fully qualified master."

According to the *shunyata* teaching of the Mahayana, everything is empty and open by nature, including both body and mind and all external phenomena. All things are selfless, ungovernable, unreliable, and impermanent. They are totally without independent self-existence or permanent individual entityness. That understanding of absolute emptiness is reached by the understanding of true selflessness, which means the nonexistence of the separate individual self and the nonexistence of the eternal self of phenomena.

Nothing can be confirmed as either existent or nonexistent, nor both nor neither. This is the profound lion's roar of Nagarjuna and his followers, who elaborated the Middle Way philosophy of Madhyamika, the supreme teaching of emptiness.

Yet isn't there a cognizance present in all this openness and emptiness, a vivid clarity or luminous awareness undeniably functioning right now and throughout all our existences? This is because the empty essence of mind, which is actually none other than dharmakaya (the formless body of absolute truth), is by nature luminous, aware, cognizant (which is the *sambhogakaya*, pure clear light or radiant energy), yet undeniably manifests unobstructedly as manifold expressions of dynamic compassion (the *nirmanakaya*, or *tulku*, the form body of enlightened activity). Understood in this way, isn't it obvious that the three *kayas* are inseparable and inherent in one's own heart-mind?

Mipham Rinpoche's *Prayer of the Ground, Path, and Fruit* says:

> Present since the beginning, it is not dependent upon being cultivated,
> Nor upon such things as differences in one's capacity.
> May this vital point of the nature of mind, hard to believe since seeming so easy,

Be recognized through the power of the master's oral
instructions.
May we be spontaneously perfected in the nature of nonaction, beyond both action and inaction.

Buddha-nature pervades all sentient beings. When the wisdom
of the Great Perfection is transferred to a being, it does not matter
if that being has a sharp or intelligent mind. Why is that? It is because that which prevents us from realizing the Great Perfection is
not that this Great Perfection is something fundamentally different or far away. If we cannot see our own eyelid, it is not because it
is far away like a distant mountain. It is very near but difficult to
see. The same is true with the nature of the mind.

MEETING RIGPA

How can we be introduced to such a nature? If we stay in a state
where we are not influenced by thoughts of the past, we do not
invite thoughts of the future, and we are not disturbed by thoughts
of the present. In the fresh instant of the present moment, there is a
wisdom free from all concepts. We should remain in this state without falling into drowsiness, without allowing our mind to with-
draw naturally or to wander to external objects.

As Jetsun Milarepa said, enlightenment lies in the very simple
ability to recognize the wisdom beyond thoughts, the space which
is in between the thoughts. But simply to glimpse this wisdom
does not suffice: we need to achieve firmness and stability. Though
all sentient beings have buddha-nature, they are like the young
infant of a king, a newborn prince. By nature he has royal blood,
he is meant to be a king, yet he does not have all the faculties
to govern the country, protect the subjects, defeat enemies, or
administrate.

It is the instruction of a teacher that will readily help: at first to
realize the view of the Great Perfection; secondly, to achieve skill
and perfect it; and thirdly, to achieve perfect stability in this realization. We should not expect instant realization. Jetsun Milarepa
said, "Do not have expectation of the fruit, but practice until death."

In the beginning we should practice often for short periods. Our
confidence in the view will gradually grow. A time will come when
certainty will be born from within. The "subject" who experiences
the practice will vanish. When the realization has fully bloomed

we will become like the omniscient Longchen Rabjam Rinpoche. We should aspire to see the vanishing point of the thoughts, because the realization of the guru will enter through that, and merge with our self.

Lama Mipham prayed:

> To elaborate or to examine is nothing but adding concepts.
> To make effort or to cultivate is only to exhaust oneself.
> To focus or to meditate is but a trap of further entanglement.
> May these dissatisfying fabrications be cut from within.

We will never come to the end of intellectual investigation. Intellectual investigation is like a small bird flying from a ship in the ocean, trying to find the limit of the sky. The sky is so vast, and the small bird's wings become so tired, that he has no choice than to come back to the ship. In the same way, if we engage in mental fabrications, we will never find an end to them. We will just tire ourselves.

The view is not something that is linked with objects, or representations, or targets. If there are such targets or representations, there is clinging. It is said, "If there is clinging then there is no view." A view mixed with clinging and representation cannot be named the Great Perfection. If we have concepts we will put appearance on one side and voidness on the other, and in no way will we come near to the realization of the Buddha's mind, the inseparability of voidness and appearances that is free from all conditions.

In this way we exhaust ourselves by searching for different methods and fabricating different exercises. We exhaust ourselves in three ways: We create fabrications like mental concepts. We exert a lot of effort. We create many objects or targets in our minds. These are the three things that really tire us. It is like an insect caught in a spider's web: the more agitated it becomes, the more tangled it gets in the web. This creates real suffering, real torment for the mind.

If we decide that there is no need for elaboration, no need for any effort, and no need for any targets, we will be able to rest in a state that is vast like sky. This is the absolute nature, in which one has rid oneself of something to be seen and a subject who sees. This is the view, the realization of the natural state of things.

Lama Mipham wrote:

Being beyond thought or description, not a thing is seen.
There is, however, nothing extra remaining to be seen.
That is the profound meaning of resolving one's mind.
May this nature, hard to illustrate, be realized.

So what is to be done to realize the natural Great Perfection, Dzogpa Chenpo, if it is free from all concepts, efforts, and representations? The *Prajnaparamita Sutra* says, "The perfection of wisdom is beyond thought." It should not be conceived of, for it is inconceivable and cannot be described. The absolute truth is not something that can be apprehended by the mind of ordinary beings. In order to indicate this to beings, in a relative way, the Buddhas have said that the void nature is like the sky, while its luminous expression is like the sun. But in truth, even a Buddha cannot entirely express the nature of the mind; there are no words or examples to explain it. It is utterly beyond the relative mind of beings. Yet it is not something that did not exist before, like a new thing appearing for the first time.

When we are free from all conceptualizations and mental fabrications we can see this nature. When Karma Chagme Rinpoche realized the absolute nature, Mahamudra, he said to his friend, "This is something that has been with me forever. It is something I have known forever. Why didn't you tell me that this was Mahamudra itself?" When we see the true nature within ourselves, there is nothing more to be seen, There is nothing more to be found in the eighty-four thousand teachings.

The *Prajnaparamita Sutra* says:

Regarding mind:
Mind does not exist,
Its expression is luminosity.

GROUND, PATH, AND FRUITION

In *The Diamond Verses of the Absolute Nature*, Rigdzin Jigme Lingpa sang:

Even if a hundred learned beings and hundreds of *siddhas*
    would claim that this view is wrong,
In this there is nothing seen to be discarded,
Nor is there anything to be kept or established.
May this state of *dharmata*, unspoiled by acceptance and
    rejection,
Be perceived as the spontaneously present nature.

> Although true nature is divided into the 'ground to be
>   known,'
> The 'path to be journeyed,' and the 'fruition to be attained,'
> These three are but like levels in open space.
> May we spontaneously abide in the nature of nonaction.

In truth, in the way things really are, from the very beginning the qualities of the essence of buddhahood—the *tathagatagarbha*— are fully bright without modification, without losing anything at all. They are present within every sentient being.

On the path, this essence of buddhahood never changes: it does not increase, nor does it decrease. It does not have to undergo any modification.

Regarding fruition again, this very essence of buddhahood that is realized is perfectly complete. There is nothing to be added to it. There is nothing more that a Buddha could discover. In fact, from the point of view of the way things are, there is no reason to make distinctions such as different *bhumis* or levels. There are no such things as a starting point, a path, and a goal. All these are like looking at the sky and trying to see different delineations, levels, or limits within it. We can make these configurations intellectually, but in truth there are no subdivisions in the sky. If we say, "This is the top of the sky and this is the bottom of the sky," it is still just the sky.

In fact, there is nothing to be done, so we may abide in *nonaction*, beyond both action and inaction. We already have this perfect unchanging nature, so why try to perfect ourselves, purify ourselves, attend to a teacher, and go along the path? This question inevitably arises.

In general, the view and meditation of the eight vehicles are somewhat adulterated by mental fabrications, but the ninth vehicle, Ati Yoga or Dzogpa Chenpo, is completely beyond intellectual activity.

A vast sky can be considered as void or luminous, but it is all one. From the aspect of essence, it is beyond such distinctions as view, meditation, and action. There is an "appearing aspect" that we may call a "view," which is to find one's own nature; a "meditation," which is to bring everything back to this single point or conviction; and an "action," which is to gain confidence through the method of spontaneously liberating thoughts.

Lama Mipham wrote:

> Whatever one is focused on is poison for the view.
> Whatever is embraced by effort is a fault of meditation.
> Whatever is adopted or abandoned is a defect of action.
> May we perceive the nature free from all shortcomings and
>   limitations.

How should this view be? The view should be completely free from clinging. As Manjushri said in a vision to the great Sakyapa teacher Trakpa Gyaltsen, "If there is clinging, there is no view." The view is completely free from conditions, concepts, and characteristics. Object, representations, targets, and postulates are like poison to the view. With these the view cannot be pure. If someone eats poison he will die immediately. In the same way, the view is spoiled by clinging to either materialism or nihilism. This becomes a cause for wandering further into samsara. Clinging in this way, we can never be free from the bondage of ego.

According to the Dzogpa Chenpo, if one engages in striving, clinging, and tense effort during one's meditation, it is a defect. One should remain in a view, meditation, and action, free from fabrication. For such a yogi, whatever he does with his body, speech, and mind—everything, even just moving his hand in the air—takes place as the display of awareness. For this reason, there is no need for an enlightened being to purposely cultivate virtuous actions or discard nonvirtuous actions. Whatever he does is within the display of wisdom.

The absolute expanse has never been stained or limited by concepts such as nirvana and samsara or existing and nonexisting. We should become enlightened like the primordial Buddha Kuntuzangpo, who was enlightened in the original ground. Aside from this very original ground of buddhahood, it is imposing hardship on ourselves to strive to achieve a spiritual state that we have always had. We have buddha-mind within, so there is no need for all these hardships; just as when someone has already reached the diamond throne at Bodhgaya in India, there is no need for them to undertake difficult travels through hard conditions in order to get there.

The primordial Buddha, the great *vidyadharas*, and all those who achieved enlightenment, merely actualized qualities they always had, they were not fabricating new qualities.

In practicing the oral pith-instructions, what we really need is to be liberated through recognizing our own awareness, the ultimate nature of being itself. This will not come through the so-called secret teachings and pith-instructions found in books. The first eight vehicles take us along the path working with the mind: none of those vehicles take wisdom itself as the path. Dzogpa Chenpo takes the wisdom itself as the path, and it is therefore devoid of any representations and objects. We need to utilize wisdom—how things actually are—as the path, not merely using our mental fabrications. Because whatever is related to the mind is automatically related to delusion, to the clinging between subject and object.

Lama Mipham wrote:

> Since the unfabricated and uncompounded dharmata
> Has nothing new to be obtained through the path of
>   fabrications,
> May the nature of the ultimate fruition, which does not
>   result from a cause,
> Be perceived as being primordially present within oneself.

Vividly present and awake, free from concepts, through constant re-mindfulness recognizing everything, wherever we are—under all circumstances and conditions—as the magical display of rigpa; seeing through everything and never falling prey to ego-clinging, attachment, and dualistic fixation, nor to its further elaborations as the three poisons (*kleshas*) and the eighty-four thousand defilements; thus we maintain our primordial throne, like the enlightened sovereign personifying intrinsic awareness, Samantabhadra.

On the other hand, being deceived by this unobstructed spontaneous magical display of intrinsic awareness itself; confused by ignorance and falling into the duality of subject and object; thus we forego our primordial throne, depart from our spiritual kingdom, and, like the prodigal son in the Bible, forget who and what we are, to wander endlessly like stray dogs lost on the endless plains of samsaric existence.

The great good fortune of meeting an authentic enlightened master and being introduced to the ultimate view—recognizing, acknowledging, confirming our true nature—is like being reintroduced to ourselves, like the prodigal son being restored to his rightful place as crown prince of his father's kingdom, beyond the possibility of doubt or disputation.

All the phenomena of samsara and nirvana are perfect and complete within rigpa. One instant of total awareness, recognition of rigpa, is enough: the *Manjushri-namasamgiti Tantra* says, "In one moment, perfect recognition, in one instant, complete enlightenment." The wisdom-mind of all the Buddhas, innate wakefulness, is inherent to our very nature, yet it is temporarily obscured by conceptuality. Innate vajra-like buddha-mind, rigpa, is unveiled the moment dualistic mind dissolves and nondual awareness nakedly dawns, which is none other than the immaculate and primordially pure dharmakaya. This is the authentic Buddha, the Buddha within. There is no Buddha apart from one's own heart-mind, as Milarepa and other siddhas often sang.

The main difference between deluded mind and enlightened mind is the degree of narrowness and openness. The essential nature being one and undivided, it is immediately apparent to those with eyes to see, the degree to which any particular individual is open, free, and unconditioned or, on the other hand, rigid, close-minded, fixated, attached, and confused—that is, totally conditioned by adventitious obscurations, the karmic imprints of previous actions and obscuring emotions and defilements.

THE ULTIMATE NATURE OF MIND

After his great awakening beneath the bodhi tree in Bodhgaya, Lord Buddha said that the ultimate nature of mind is perfectly pure, profound, quiescent, luminous, uncompounded, unconditioned, unborn and undying, and free since the beginningless beginning. When we examine this mind for ourselves, it becomes apparent that its innate openness, clarity, and cognizant quality comprise what is known as innate wakefulness, primordial nondual awareness: rigpa. This is our birthright, our true nature. It is not something missing, to be sought for and obtained, but is the very heart of our original existential being. It is actually inseparable from our uncontrived everyday awareness, beyond willful alteration, free from conceptuality: unfabricated ordinary awareness, unadulterated by effort and modification—naked, fresh, vivid, and totally natural. What could be simpler than this, to rest at home and at ease in total naturalness?

The sutra vehicles, the common teachings of Buddhadharma, consider that the above-mentioned description of the ultimate nature of mind by Lord Buddha himself refers to nirvana, or nirvanic consciousness. According to the Vajrayana practice lineages of Tibet, and especially the Mahamudra and Dzogchen traditions, that description refers to the true nature of mind, rigpa, intrinsic awareness itself. In that light, how far is that fabled "other shore," nirvana?

So get out of the construction business! Stop building bridges across the raging waters of samsaric existence, attempting to reach the "far shore," nirvana. Better to simply relax, at ease and carefree, in total naturalness, and just go with the primordial flow, however it occurs and happens. And remember this: whether or not you go with the flow, it always goes with you.

Yet it is not so easy—or so it seems. First we must recognize this profound view, innate Great Perfection, then train in it, then attain unshakable stability in it. This is the path of practice, undistractedly maintaining the view or outlook to which one has been introduced and which one has recognized. Only then can realization progressively unfold. Thus, training implies nonmeditation, noneffort, and nondistraction, a vivid presence of mind. Innate wakefulness, nonconceptual wisdom, nondual primordial awareness—buddha-mind—is suddenly unsheathed the moment dualistic mind dissolves. This can occur gradually, through study, analysis, and spiritual practice, or suddenly, through the coming together of causes and conditions, such as when a ripe student encounters a totally realized master and inexplicably experiences a sudden awakening.

Buddha-nature is pure, undefiled, unelaborated, unconditioned, transcending all concepts. It is not an object of dualistic thought and intellectual knowledge. It is, however, open to gnosis, intuition, the nondual apperception of intrinsic awareness itself, prior to or upstream of consciousness. Adventitious obscurations temporarily veil and, like clouds, obscure this pristine, sky-like, luminous fundamental nature or mind essence—also known as tathagatagarbha, buddha-nature.

All conventional practices along the gradual path to liberation and enlightenment aim to uncover this innate wisdom by removing and dissolving the obscurations, revealing what has always been present. This is the relation between how things appear to be and how things actually are: in short, the two levels of truth, absolute and relative or conventional truth. According to these two truths, there are different levels of practice.

The subtle and profound Vajrayana view emphasizes correctly recognizing the ultimate view, the wisdom inherent within oneself; this is the renowned vajra-shortcut elucidated in the Dzogchen tantras. The approach of the various sutra vehicles depends on, and utilizes, purification of dualistic consciousness, until the mind is eventually purified and freed of obscurations and defilements. The tantric approach depends upon, and from the outset utilizes, wisdom, nondual awareness, rather than mere mind. This is a crucial difference.

The sublime view of Dzogpa Chenpo, the ultimate vehicle, is that everything is pure and perfect from the outset. This is the absolute truth, the supreme outlook or view of Buddhas, which implies that there is nothing that need be done or accomplished. Based on such recognition of how things actually are, the meditation of Dzogchen is nonmeditation, resting in the evenness of *being*, rather than doing any particular thing, beyond hope and fear, adopting and rejecting. The action or behavior of Dzogchen ensues from such transcendence, and is totally spontaneous, aimless, and appropriate to whatever conditions arise. The fruition of Dzogchen is the innate Great Perfection itself, inseparable from the very starting point of this swift and efficacious path: rigpa itself, one's own true nature.

The famous enlightened vagabond, the nineteenth century Dzogchen master Patrul Rinpoche, sang, "Beyond both action and inaction, the supreme Dharma is accomplished. So simply preserve the natural state and rest your weary mind." His compassionate, humble lifestyle and profound writings are still widely studied today, inspiring practitioners of all the sects and lineages of Tibet.

Padampa Sangye said, "Everything is found within the natural state, so do not seek elsewhere." Buddhahood is the wisdom within us all, it is not elsewhere. It is actually our fundamental nature, the primordial state, our inherent freedom and unfabricated beingness.

That is why it is called the natural state, innate buddha-nature, and said to be possessed by all beings. This is the *raison d'etre* of Dzogpa Chenpo, the natural Great Perfection. There is nothing beyond or superior to this. Realize it, as it is—even right now—and everything is included. All wishes and aspirations are fulfilled in this natural state of innate wakefulness, our own innate great perfection, Dzogchen. It belongs to each and every one of us.

Different purposes or approaches give it different names, depending on whether it is being seen as the view, the goal, the practice path, the fundamental ground, or otherwise. This single ineffable essence is variously known as tathagatagarbha, *sugata-garbha*, buddha-nature, rigpa, empty and cognizant self-existing wakefulness, dharmakaya, Prajnaparamita, transcendental wisdom, shunyata or emptiness, clear light, buddha-mind, and so on. Rigpa—whether called intrinsic awareness, nondual presence, self-existing inherent wisdom, or innate wakefulness—is like one's own individual share of the transpersonal ultimate body of truth, the dharmakaya of all the Buddhas. There is nothing superior to this.

Chokyi Nyima Rinpoche said, "The enlightened essence (buddha-nature) is present within the heart-mind of every sentient being. Dzogchen directly introduces and reveals how this actually is, unbarring the natural state. The pith-instructions show how it can be nakedly recognized within one's own experience. They note the great need for recognizing it and the tremendous benefit of doing so, clearly showing how, at that very moment, the Buddha, the awakened state, need not be sought for elsewhere, but is present within oneself, and that you become enlightened through experiencing what was always present within you. This is the effect of *nyongtri*, instruction through personal experience."

As Asanga and Maitreya said, the nature of mind is luminous. It is perfectly empty, open, and aware, unfettered by conditions or conditioning. The mind, or dualistic consciousness, is a mere impermanent concatenation of causes and conditions, totally bound up in conditioning. The difference between mind and its nature—the difference between awareness or mind-essence, and conceptual thinking or *namtok*—is like the difference between the sky or space itself, and the ephemeral weather which occurs within it. In the *Prajnaparamita Sutra* Buddha says, "True mind is not the dual-istic mind. The nature of mind is actually the inseparability of awareness and emptiness."

Longchenpa says that mind is duality, that rigpa, nondual aware-ness, is transcendental wisdom. The fundamental nature of mind is sheer lucency, free and unfettered by concepts such as subject and object; a profound luminosity free from partiality and fixa-tion, a free-flowing compassionate expression of indefinable, lim-itless emptiness, unobscured by thinking. Thought is bondage; the immeasurable openness of empty awareness is freedom. Compas-sion for those bound within their own illusory constructs, mind-forged manacles, and self-imposed limitations, spontaneously, unobstructedly, and inexhaustibly springs forth.

Therefore, with the essential pith-instructions of a qualified Dzogchen master, crush the eggshell of the mind and unfold your wings in the open sky. Destroy the hut of duality and inhabit the expansive mansion of rigpa. There are no other enemies or ob-stacles to overcome and vanquish. Ignorance—dualistic thinking—is the great demon obstructing your path. Slay it right now and be free.

5 Dzogchen and the Buddhism of Tibet

A Teaching in Cambridge, Massachusetts

This group is called the Dzogchen Foundation or the Cambridge
Dzogchen Group. It's easy to receive a name like that, but it is a
huge name to live up to—Dzogchen, the innate Great Perfection.
However, please don't think I mean to say that it is something that
you don't already possess. That is why I have offered you such a
name.

I exhort you to practice well this sublime way of awakening
called Dzogchen, the Great Perfection. This is the very heart of the
vast and profound Dharma taught by the enlightened one, Lord
Buddha. The heart of the enlightened one's teachings is the precious bodhicitta, the altruistic enlightened heart and mind. This
could also be called love and compassion. It has two aspects: absolute bodhicitta and relative bodhicitta. The basic teachings of Buddhism—the root vehicle taught in the Sutras, Vinaya, and
Abhidharma—stress very much the need for renunciation, or the
arising of certainty regarding the illusory nature of things, impermanence, selflessness, and the dissatisfactory nature of all conditioned phenomena. These are the basic teachings of Buddhism. The
later Mahayana teachings stress empathy, love, and compassion.

The preliminary practices, the *ngondros*, mind training, and so
on, all form a firm foundation to cultivate basic insights into, and
awareness of, the basic teachings. They form a broad, stable foundation or basis to develop bodhicitta, the awakened heart-mind,
the luminous heart of the Great Perfection.

In the Mahayana teaching it is explained that great emptiness endowed with luminous compassion is our true nature. That is what we cultivate in the relative bodhicitta teachings; and that is what we realize has always been inseparable from us, according to the absolute bodhicitta teachings.

Whichever side of the bodhicitta we are emphasizing—the relative cultivation of enlightened qualities for the benefit of relieving the suffering of all; or the absolute side, the immanent or self-present, existing self-nature of things, great emptiness endowed with luminosity or compassion—both sides need to be completed or balanced to have a fully developed practice. In the Vajrayana teachings, the absolute bodhicitta is very clearly articulated in the pith-instructions—the personal advice—of how to recognize it directly without any theoretical explorations or analyses; directly through the blessings and transmission of the practice lineage, the way of practice and experience.

Whatever you call it, however we aspire or understand it, from the point of view of absolute or relative truths, Great Vehicle or Small Vehicle, it is the same liberating teaching, the heart of the Buddhist teaching. It is like if you have tuberculosis, almost any doctor can diagnose it. Whether you take the medicine in the morning, in the afternoon, or at night, it will cure the disease. Similarly, with the Buddhist teachings, with this teaching about bodhicitta, whether you practice the absolute bodhicitta, the great paths of Mahamudra, Dzogchen, and Madhyamika, the nondual teachings; or whether you emphasize the relative bodhicitta, through the developmental practices and more gradual vehicles—each of these is all-inclusive and converges on the same principle, the experience of great liberation and perfect fulfillment, nirvanic peace.

Of all the Buddhist teachings, the main thing is the release or loosening of selfishness, of self-grasping, of ego-cherishing, of craving, resistance and attachment. That directly leads to the alleviation of suffering, the end of dissatisfactoriness, because grasping or egotism is the main cause of suffering. There are many different ways of explaining the paths, the antidotes, the transformations, the purifications, the visionary experiences, the different results of different kinds of practices; but in general, what has been explained here is the heart of the practice. We don't need to proliferate too many different studies and thinking. Simply loosen egotism and attachment, open the heart and mind, and enjoy inner joy, peace, and unselfish love. Do it for one and all!

It is very important in the Buddhist spiritual way to rely on a *kalyanamitra*, a spiritual friend, a teacher. The Buddha, through many lifetimes, relied on spiritual teachers. He didn't attain perfect awakened Buddhahood just in one lifetime through a few years of meditation, but rather through many lifetimes of aspirations, prayers, practice, and receiving teachings and guidance. Without the clarifications and guidance of a teacher, it is very difficult to genuinely experience the truth of the teachings. Without teachings, it is very difficult to genuinely experience freedom and enlightenment through practice alone. A teacher can guide us. A qualified teacher has the experience to prevent one from deviations and pitfalls. A teacher can find the most direct way for the student. If one aspires to realize the teachings of the innate Great Perfection, one might very well aspire to receive teachings and to practice the *guru yoga*, in which one realizes the inseparability of oneself and the enlightened teacher. According to the Dzogchen tradition, the entire Dharma can be explained in the context of this form of practice, guru yoga, devotion. This kind of devotion can bring realization of the beginningless inseparability of our heart and mind and the buddha-mind.

The Dzogchen teachings are an extremely vast and profound treasury. The Buddha taught eighty-four thousand Dharma teachings, classified into three vehicles or *yanas*. The third of these, the Vajrayana (Tantrayana) is further subdivided into four (or six) Tantrayanas. Then there are outer teachings, inner teachings, hidden or so-called secret teachings. And yet all of these are realized through the devotion and wisdom practice found in the guru yoga, the mingling of the practitioner and the guru's nature.

Maybe you think that a teacher has a body or bones or hair, or that you need one hair of the teacher, or a red protection cord, to get blessings. That's the relative teacher. If you really want to know what the guru means, the guru is the entire self-arising phenomenal universe. It is like an example, the symbolic master. It's not the human teacher that is the master. Truth is every single momentary arising, the entire phenomenal universe. The absolute guru or teacher is the nature of all things. Don't think it is just some old man, some lama or guru figure. There is the *nirmanakaya*, the manifest lama, like the Buddha in human form, the living teacher. There is the *sambhogakaya*, the energy, the mystical guru manifesting as experience: the true nature of our own experience, the inner guru. Then there is the most formless, absolute guru: the *dharmakaya*, the great luminous emptiness. All of these can be realized in one moment of great resting of pure awareness, the great letting go of all things, called the *yeshe lama*, the wisdom, the gnostic master or the inner guru, the great leaving-it-as-it-is.

If you want to go even further, there is the infinitely radiant-from-within nature of all things that is like a total Buddha-blessing manifesting everywhere. The thusness guru, *isness*. Everything that is in this Dzogchen collection, this treasure-house, this *mandala*, is actually the display or the energy of the enlightened guru or the buddha-mind. All animate and inanimate existence and all experiences, outer and inner, are actually the Buddha, the true teacher. If you understand the Great Perfection teachings, every moment these blessings pour forth. One is never apart from the true guru, the Buddha, one's own primordial nature.

If you just hear the words "Dzogchen" or "Dzogpa Chenpo," the innate natural Great Perfection, it is very easy to say, "Oh, yes. I know what that means. Dzogpa Chenpo means Great Perfection." It is easy to say that, only a few syllables. No doubt all of you have experienced teachings and blessings from many teachers, many gurus, many lamas. You have received these profound blessings. If you really recognized your ultimate inseparability from the Buddha, inseparability from the teacher in every situation and every moment, then that is the absolute principle of Dzogpa Chenpo—not just knowing that the words mean Great Perfection.

That is why we shouldn't overlook the importance of the guru yoga practice when we want to approach the true Dzogchen practice. Devotion swiftly cuts through discursivity. That is the threshold that opens the mansion of nonduality, of inseparability. When one realizes the blessings that are always pouring forth, that is the moment of Dzogchen. There is no other moment, initiation, or teaching. Then all of existence, animate and inanimate, outer and inner, are truly realized as the innate Great Perfection, Dzogchen. There is no other Dzogchen to request, to study, or to practice. There are many teachers in the lineage throughout history coming down to us. There is also the primordial lama or guru, which is the nature of everything, including ourselves: the true lineage master, which we are never separate from. In order to receive teachings or to realize that, the guru yoga is very, very effective and profound: realizing the inseparability of oneself and the enlightened teacher, the Buddha.

If you think that the lama is a person, then you might think that the Buddha is a statue made out of wood; then the whole thing starts to get further and further away, as if the Buddha is up there on the altar, the lama is up there on the dais, and one is just a spectator. Then, if you are in a house or in the mountains, you won't find your guru there. It could be very frustrating if you foolishly push it away from yourself like that, for the guru-principle manifests everywhere.

It is said that everything is magically self-appearing, or spontaneously manifests; that everything is unborn and deathless. Moreover, it is said that the blessings of the three jewels—the Buddha, Dharma, and Sangha—are always pouring down. However, it depends on our devotion to connect, or open, to it. It is said that everything is karmic perception; in other words, how we experience the world depends on how we perceive it, depends on our own karma. It is like our projection. There are many discussions in the sutras and commentaries about impermanence and particles and atoms, and analyzing it further down to emptiness, and then emptiness also being empty, ad infinitum. Analyzing it further, we reach down towards nothing, and even beyond nothing. All of these things are karmic perception, our own projection, conceptual imputations upon reality.

Dzogchen does not point to anything. It is beyond all delusory, dualistic perceptions and projections. Beyond delusion, everything is perfect. Within delusion, everything seems to be not great perfection. When there is no deception or delusion, this here in my hand is obviously a flower. Some deluded person might perceive it as water, but that would be a delusion or mistake. When one sees things as they are—as in this example, the flower right in front of us—the entire external phenomenal and internal noumenal universe is the great Dzogpa Chenpo, the great buddha-nature, the Great Perfection. When one is undeluded, when things are seen as they are, everything is the display of energy of the buddha-nature, the radiance of reality, the Great Perfection.

One can be even more deluded, and think that Dharma teachings aren't true, that the Buddha is just a myth and so on. You might think, for example, that this is not the Great Perfection, that this is not Dzogpa Chenpo here, this is just Boston. Or you might be still more deluded and you might think this is not Dzogpa Chenpo, this is New York! Different shades of delusion. You might have a different brand of delusion and think, this is not the Great Perfection, Dzogpa Chenpo. This is John translating, not Surya Das. Delusion upon delusion!

Dzogpa Chenpo is how things actually are. Things left just as they are. The natural state. How things actually are, their true mode of being. The great knowledge holder, lineage master Jigme Lingpa, the fearless master who lived three hundred years ago in Tibet, said, "Teachings about Dzogchen are many. Knowers of Dzogchen are few." My own precious root lama, the great Khenpo Ngawang Palzang, disciple of Patrul Rinpoche, the great Dzogchen master, said, "Dzogchen is extremely simple, but not easy." It is easy for anybody to point to the sky. It is easy for anybody to say something about Dzogchen and how everything is perfect in its true nature. But most people see the finger and they don't see the sky. So if you see the finger and you didn't see the sky, then there is ngondro, refuge, bodhicitta practice, a lot of meditations and purifications to do in order to purify and dispel the obscurations temporarily obscuring our buddha-nature, our own true nature. But don't look at the sky through a straw—the straw of your own limited viewpoint—and think that is all there is to the infinite vastness of space.

When a mirror is cloudy or dusty, if it is polished, its true nature—its lucidity and reflective brilliance—shines forth. Just to say that it is perfect already won't help very much if it is covered by obscurations.

What else is there to say? We already wasted a few minutes here. So please take up this practice if it makes sense to you. Put yourself into it through prayer and devotion, through meditation and self-inquiry. Spiritual practice is a very personal thing, so it is up to you. Take the opportunity. Bring it into your own day-to-day life.

The great Dzogchen patriarch, the omniscient Buddha Longchenpa, six hundred years ago simply summed it up in two words in Tibetan. He said, *"Semnyi ngalso!"*—"Great ease!" Natural ease of mind. He didn't say natural busyness of mind. He said natural peace or ease of mind. Therefore, ease into it. Let go and drop everything. We don't need to think a lot about understanding these things. This is something that can be experienced or recognized from within, in a different way. When we meditate, we don't need to use the mind very much. We can ease simply into the natural ease of being. Open to effortless, innate awareness, not just trying to control the mind but actually appreciating and seeing it as it is.

There are many different ways of meditating and practicing. Some of them are analytical and very helpful in sharpening the mind, in discriminating and discerning things clearly. There are many who understand and realize that very well. But our tradition is more the experiential lineage, the practice lineage of the union of the Mahamudra and Dzogchen nondual streams, the inseparability of wisdom and compassion, *prajna* and *upaya*, truth and love, as a method for awakening.

This includes both *shamatha* (calm abiding) and *vipashyana* (insight) in the form of panoramic awareness meditation. It includes analytical discernment. It includes resting in the natural state, in openness and ease. There are many different capacities or inclinations of beings, so there are many different approaches or facets of this single liberating jewel. They are all a single, coherent approach. In the ultimate, one can only say that immanent wisdom is directly, nakedly present; self-existing wakefulness is never apart from us. What is there to be distracted from, in the light of pure and total presence? How can we ever be far from it?

Please recognize this innate wisdom, this self-existing awareness, this great buddha-nature. This is the purpose of practice. Not just to keep looking for it, but to actually recognize it and realize it in oneself, for the limitless benefit and joy of one and all.

Today has been a kind of essentialized or condensed version of the teaching. If you are interested in these things, feel free to pursue them with Lama Surya Das or with other teachers for days, months, or years. It looks like you are all staying in America and you are not going anywhere, and Surya is staying in America, so make the most of it; he is fully trained, empowered and authorized by myself and his other teachers.

The Great Perfection teachings have been around for thousands of years. It is not something that the Tibetans invented. It's been around for a long time. The Dzogchen masters brought it from India, but even before that, it was around.

Buddhism and these teachings became more and more obscure in India, lost in India, but were carried on in Tibet and in surrounding countries by the people of those countries, who received the teachings from Indian teachers and then practiced, realized, and established them in their own countries until today. For thirteen hundred years the Tibetans have made great efforts to preserve and uphold these sublime and profound teachings. Until now they have not let them disappear. They practiced them, and people have realized enlightenment. They translated them. They did everything they could to preserve, practice, and realize these precious teachings. Suddenly they are being offered to the whole world, pervading the whole world, for the benefit of all. This is the moment of Dzogchen.

The Dharma is like pure elixir, like nectar. Naturally, one feels like preserving it, cherishing it, safeguarding it, and sharing it. If nobody appreciates it, then these words are just like mist dissolving in the air, lost, gone. On the other hand, if those who hear these things take them up, practice them, and realize them, then they get the full benefit of these truths. They are for everybody. They are to be transmitted and passed on. There is no question about secrecy, about protecting them, about keeping them back. They must proliferate and continue.

Spiritual practice benefits all. It benefits the individual. It benefits the community. It benefits the country. It benefits the universe. It benefits all, and blesses all.

Spiritual practice is extremely important. Please appreciate it.

Praying to omniscient Longchenpa: May your wisdom mind and ours remain inseparable.

Homage to the innate Great Perfection. May all realize and embody it!

This talk was given to the Cambridge Dzogchen Group at Kunkyab Rangjung Yeshe Ling, June 8, 1994.

Songs and Commentary

A formal portrait of Nyoshul Khenpo Rinpoche Jamyang Dorje performing a Vajrayana empowerment. Photo courtesy of Khenpo Sonam Tobgyal Rinpoche.

6 The Mirror of Essential Points

*A Letter in Praise of Emptiness, from Khenpo
Jamyang Dorje to His Mother*

Translated by Erik Hein Schmidt and edited by Ani Lodrö
Palmo and Ward Brisick

I pay homage at the lotus feet of Tenpai Nyima,
Who is inseparable from Dharma-lord Longchen Rabjam,
And perceives the natural state of emptiness
Of the ocean-like infinity of things.

A letter of advice I offer to you, my noble mother Paldzom.
Listen for a while without distraction.

Staying here without discomfort,
I am at ease and free from worries,
In a state of joyful mind.
Are you well yourself, my dear mother?

Here, in a country to the west,
There are many red- and white-skinned people.
They have all kinds of magic and sights,
Like flying through the skies,
And moving like fish in the waters.
Having mastery over the four elements,
They compete in displaying miracles
With thousands of beautiful colors.

There is an endless amount of spectacles,
Like designs of rainbow colors,
But like a mere dream, when examined,
They are the mistaken perceptions of the mind.

All activities are like the games children play.
If done, they can never be finished.
They are only completed once you let be,
Like castles made of sand.

But this is not the whole story.
All the *dharmas* of samsara and nirvana,
Though thought to be permanent, they do not last.
When examined, they are but empty forms
That appear without existence.
Although unreal, they are thought to be real,
And when examined, they are unreal like an illusion.

Look outward at the appearing objects,
And like the water in a mirage,
They are more delusive than delusion.
Unreal like dreams and illusions,
They resemble a reflected moon and rainbows.

Look inward at your own mind!
It seems quite exciting, when not examined.
But when examined, there is nothing to it.
Appearing without being, it is nothing but empty.
It cannot be identified saying, "That's it!"
But is evanescent and elusive like mist.

Look at whatever may appear
In any of the ten directions.
No matter how it may appear,
The thing in itself, its very nature,
Is the sky-like nature of mind,
Beyond the projection and dissolution of thought and concept.

Everything has the nature of being empty.
When the empty looks at the empty,
Who is there to look at something empty?

What is the use of many classifications,
Such as "being empty" and "not empty,"
As it is illusion looking at illusion,
And delusion watching delusion?

"The effortless and sky-like nature of the mind,
The vast expanse of insight,
Is the natural state of all things.
In it, whatever you do is all right,
However you rest, you are at ease."
This was said by Jetsun Padmasambhava,
And the great siddha Saraha.

All the conceptual designs,
Such as "It's two!" or "It's not two!"
Leave them like the waves on a river,
To be spontaneously freed in themselves.

The great demon of ignorant and discursive thought
Causes one to sink in the ocean of samsara.
But when freed from this discursive thought,
There is the indescribable state, beyond conceptual mind.

Besides mere discursive thoughts,
There is not even the words *samsara* and *nirvana*.
The total calming down of discursive thought
Is the suchness of *dharmadhatu*.

Not made complex by complex statements,
This unfabricated single *bindu*
Is emptiness, the natural state of mind.
So it was said by the Sugata, Buddha himself.

The essence of whatever may appear,
When simply left to itself,
Is the unfabricated and uncorrupted view,
The *dharmakaya*, emptiness mother.
All discursive thought is emptiness,
And the seer of the emptiness is discursive thought.
Emptiness does not destroy discursive thought,
And discursive thought does not block emptiness.

The fourfold emptiness of the mind itself
Is the ultimate of everything.
Profound and tranquil, free from complexity,
Uncompounded luminous clarity,
Beyond the mind of conceptual ideas:
This is the depth of the mind of the Victorious Ones.

In this there is not a thing to be removed,
Nor anything that needs to be added.
It is merely the immaculate,
Looking naturally at itself.

In short, when the mind has fully severed
The fetters of clinging to something,
All the points are condensed therein.
This is the tradition of the supreme being Tilopa,
And of the great pandita Naropa.

Such a profound natural state as this
Is, among all the kinds of bliss,
The wisdom of great bliss.
Among all kinds of delight,
It is the king of supreme delight.
It is the supreme fourth empowerment,
Of all the tantric sections of the secret mantras.
It is the ultimate pointing-out instruction.

The view of "samsara and nirvana inseparable,"
And that of Mahamudra, of Dzogchen, the Middle Way and
    others,
Have many various titles,
But only one essential meaning.
This is the view of Lama Mipham.

As an aid to this king of views
One should begin with bodhicitta,
And conclude with dedication.

In order to cut off through skillful means
The fixation on an ego, the root of samsara,
The king of all great methods
Is the unsurpassable bodhicitta.

The king of perfect dedication
Is the means for increasing the roots of virtue.
This is the special teaching of Shakyamuni,
Which is not found with other teachers.

To accomplish complete enlightenment,
More than this is not necessary,
But less than this will be incomplete.
This swift path of the three excellences,
Called the heart, eye, and life-force,
Is the approach of Longchen Rabjam.

Emptiness, the wish-fulfilling jewel,
Is unattached generosity.
It is uncorrupted discipline.
It is angerless patience.
It is undeluded exertion.
It is undistracted meditation.
It is the essence of *prajna*.
It is the meaning in the three *yanas*.

Emptiness is the natural state of mind.
Emptiness is the nonconceptual refuge.
Emptiness is the absolute bodhicitta.
Emptiness is the Vajrasattva of absolving evils.
Emptiness is the *mandala* of perfect accumulations.
Emptiness is the *guru yoga* of dharmakaya.

To abide in the natural state of emptiness
Is the "calm abiding" of *shamatha*,
And to perceive it vividly clear
Is the "clear seeing" of *vipashyana*.

The view of the perfect development stage,
The wisdom of bliss and emptiness in the completion stage,
The nondual Great Perfection,
And the single bindu of dharmakaya,
All these are included within it.

Emptiness purifies the karmas.
Emptiness dispels the obstructing forces.
Emptiness tames the demons.
Emptiness accomplishes the deities.

The profound state of emptiness
Dries up the ocean of passion.
It crumples the mountain of anger.
It illuminates the darkness of stupidity.
It calms down the gale of jealousy.
It defeats the illness of the *kleshas*.
It is a friend in sorrow.
It destroys conceit in joy.
It conquers in the battle with samsara.
It annihilates the four *maras*.
It turns the eight worldly dharmas into the same taste.
It subdues the demon of ego-fixation.
It turns negative conditions into aids.
It turns bad omens into good luck.
It causes to manifest complete enlightenment.
It gives birth to the Buddhas of the three times.
Emptiness is the dharmakaya mother.

There is no teaching higher than emptiness.
There is no teaching swifter than emptiness.
There is no teaching more excellent than emptiness.
There is no teaching more profound than emptiness.

Emptiness is the "knowing of one that frees all."
Emptiness is the supreme king of medicines.
Emptiness is the nectar of immortality.
Emptiness is spontaneous accomplishment beyond effort.
Emptiness is enlightenment without exertion.

By meditating emptiness
One feels tremendous compassion
Towards the beings obscured, like ourselves, by the belief in a self,
And bodhicitta arises without effort.

All qualities of the path and *bhumis*
Will appear naturally without any effort,
And one will feel a heartfelt conviction
Regarding the law of the infallible effect of actions.

If one has but one moment of certainty
In this kind of emptiness,
The tight chain of ego-clinging
Will shatter into pieces.
This was said by Aryadeva.

More supreme than offering to the Sugatas and their sons
All the infinite buddha-fields,
Filled with the offering of gods and men,
Is to meditate on emptiness.

If the merit of resting evenly
Just for an instant in this natural state
Would take on concrete form,
Space could not contain it.

The peerless lord of the sages, Shakyamuni,
For the sake of this profound emptiness,
Threw his body into pyres of fire,
Gave away his head and limbs,
And performed hundreds of other austerities.

Although you fill the world with huge mounds
Of presents of gold and jewels,
This profound teaching on emptiness,
Even when searched for, is hard to find.
This is said in the *Hundred Thousand Verse Prajnaparamita*.

To meet this supreme teaching
Is the splendid power of merit
Of many eons beyond count.

In short, by means of emptiness,
One is, for the benefit of oneself,
Liberated into the expanse of the unborn dharmakaya,
The manifest complete enlightenment
Of the four *kayas* and the five wisdoms.
The unobstructed display of the *rupakaya*
Will then ceaselessly arise to teach whoever is in need,
By stirring the depths of samsara for the benefit of others,
Through constant, all-pervading spontaneous activity.
In all the sutras and tantras this is said
To be the ultimate fruition.

How can someone like me put into words
All the benefits and virtues hereof,
When the Victorious One, with his *vajra* tongue,
Cannot exhaust them, even if he speaks for an eon?

The glorious lord, the supreme teacher,
Who gives the teachings on emptiness,
Appears in the form of a human being,
But his mind is truly a Buddha.

Without deceit and hypocrisy,
Supplicate him from your very heart,
And without needing any other expedient,
You will attain enlightenment in this very life.
This is the manner of the all-embodying jewel,
Which is taught in the tantras of the Great Perfection.
When you have this jewel in the palm of your hand,
Do not let it meaninglessly go to waste.

Like the stars in the sky, learning
Will never come to an end through studies.
What is the use of all the various kinds
Of the many teachings requested and received?
What is the use of any practice that is higher than emptiness?

Do not aim at having many ascetic costumes,
Such as carrying a staff and wearing braids and animal skins.
Leaving the elephant back in your house,
Do not go searching for its footprints in the mountains.

Mother, meditate the essence of the mind,
As it is taught by the guru, the vajra holder,
And you will have the essence of the essence
Of all the eighty-four thousand teachings.
It is the heart nectar of a billion
Learned and accomplished ones.
It is the ultimate practice.

This advice from the core of the heart
Of the fallen monk, Jamyang Dorje,
Is the purest of the pure essence
From the bindu of my life blood.
Therefore keep it in your heart, mother.

These few words of heart advice
Were written in a beautiful countryside,
The city of the spacious blue sky,
Rivaling the splendor of divine realms.

To the devoted Chokyi Nodzom,
My dear and loving mother,
And to my own devoted students,
I offer this letter of advice.

This letter to my students was composed by one who goes by the name "Khenpo," the Tibetan, Jamyang Dorje, in the Dordogne Herbal Valley of Great Bliss, in the country of France, beyond the great ocean in the western direction.
    May virtue and auspiciousness ensue!

7 Khenpo Comments on "The Mirror of Essential Points: A Letter in Praise of Emptiness"

Translated and edited by Surya Das

"The Mirror of Essential Points" is a spontaneous vajra song, a doha, a song of enlightenment—a contemporary example of the living oral tradition stemming back to the accomplished siddhas of ancient India. Khenpo chanted it one day during a three-year retreat in Dordogne, France, between 1980 and 1984. Later it was recorded, then transcribed in Tibetan and sent to his mother in India. Later again, the Padmakara Translation Group put the song into English and French.

Whenever we undertake any form of spiritual teaching, practice, or study, it is useful and extraordinarily meaningful to generate and genuinely affirm the precious bodhicitta with both its relative and absolute aspects: to clearly motivate ourselves so that whatever we do here is for the benefit and ultimate enlightenment of all beings everywhere. Of course, our own self is included in that, so there is no need to further our habitual self-centeredness by concerning ourselves particularly with our own liberation at this point. Simply generate the precious bodhicitta and trust in that greatness of heart and openness of mind. Everything is included.

What does it mean to benefit all beings everywhere? In the relative sense it could mean to practice the six perfections and provide beings with whatever they want and need, such as material things, protection, medicine, longevity, security, and happiness, as well as Dharma teachings and assistance in spiritual practice.

In the absolute sense it could mean to sever the root of samsara and nirvana, to cut through the root of duality, of dualistic clinging, of clinging to the reality of things. This is the final benefit, the ultimate benefit, so-called Buddhahood, which means awakening or totally unfolding the heart-mind. *Sem kye* in Tibetan means bodhicitta, the altruistic awakening mind; literally it means blossoming of mind, the ultimate opening or unfolding of heart and mind.

What is the root of all dissatisfaction, frustration, and suffering? What is the root cause of *dukkha*—suffering, and imbalance? It is dualistic clinging. Attachment, resistance, and fixation are dukkha's cause. It all stems from ignorance. Dualistic clinging occurs at the meeting point of the grasper and the grasped. It is the clinging to the concrete reality of things; being deceived by mere appearances; not seeing their insubstantiality or hollowness, their emptiness and unreality. When this is seen through, clinging and attachment dry up. Then what suffering can there be? And who is there to suffer? Freedom and expansive ease are right there.

When the root of duality—dualistic clinging, dualistic perceptions, deluded perceptions—is severed, all the leaves, the branches, and even the tree trunk of samsara and nirvana naturally wither on their own and topple in their own time. Then this great spreading tree of samsara and nirvana, of duality, of worldliness, of conditioned being, does not need to be chopped down: it is already as if dead. We can relax; done is what had to be done, as the Buddha sang.

This is the whole point of the Dharma, of spiritual awakening, of Buddhahood; this is its ultimate evolution or unfolding. If we aspire to experience such an awakening, there is nothing else to do except recognize the true nature of our primordial awareness, our own essential being, our own birthright, which is within. This is the intrinsic nature of our own heart-mind, also known as bodhicitta or bodhi-mind. It is our own being, our own nature, this renowned buddha-nature. It is not a Buddha anywhere else.

That is why we say the Buddha is within: the buddha-nature pervades and embraces all beings, without exception. More profoundly, that is why we say there is no Buddha outside of our own mind, for buddha-mind is the true essence of our own mind, even now. It is not very far away at all. It is in us and is us, our true nature. But who recognizes and actualizes that? Don't we continually overlook it? It seems too good to be true, so we don't believe it. It is too close, so we overlook it. It is so manifestly evident, always, that we fail to notice it. Who can acknowledge that Buddha within themselves?

This teaching is in the form of a song about the various aspects of emptiness or *shunyata*: the effulgent void, the infinite openness of untrammeled primordial being itself. It is taught that there are eighteen different kinds of shunyata, yet all are included in one, called *mahashunyata*, great emptiness: the inconceivable openness and emptiness, the indescribable suchness of being. It is not something relative—everything else is relative; mahashunyata is the true nature of all relative phenomena.

The *Heart Sutra* says, "Form is emptiness, and emptiness is form." This is the basic Mahayana Buddhist view of reality and existence. We cannot deny that we experience the world, an infinite variety of appearances and existences. Yet in essence, all things are empty of intrinsic reality, of substantial, independent existence. This is what is meant by shunyata, emptiness. This is the union of the two levels of truth, relative and absolute. A Buddha perceives both simultaneously: how things appear to be—the relative or functional level, and how things actually are.

Shunyata is the absolute truth, the true nature of all things, their fundamental mode of being. The true condition of all phenomena, of both samsara and nirvana, is mahashunyata, the great openness or emptiness. This is the true meaning of Dzogpa Chenpo, the natural great completion teachings, the inherent purity and perfection of all things: that all things are characterized by mahashunyata, great openness or emptiness.

One might wonder: Who or what created, fabricated, made this emptiness, this great openness, which is the natural state of all the phenomena of samsara and nirvana? Did the Buddha make it? Did some god or absolute being create it? Did beings construct it? Is it made or born from anywhere? Is it what remains when everything is purified or annihilated? Do we have to remove the veil of thought and concept in order to perceive it?

Shunyata is unborn, unmade, and uncreated. Therefore it is said to be undying, like nirvana (which Buddha himself called eternal in a sutra). It is the true nature, the ultimate nature—mahashunyata, great emptiness. Inconceivable, yes; impossible, no!

The nature of all phenomena, as the Lord Buddha said, is impermanent. All things fall apart. Whatever is born, dies. All those who have gathered together are dispersed, just like meetings in a marketplace. All constructions are eventually ruined. All conditioned phenomena are impermanent, ungovernable, selfless, and empty, like a dream, mirage, echoes. Amazing! Wonderful! *Emaho!*

The true nature of things itself is mahashunyata, the great openness or emptiness, the ultimate relativity free from independent, individual existent entities—unborn, undying, immutable, inconceivable, beyond conceptualization. It is the absolute truth. It can never fall apart. It is beyond time and space. It is not a thing, an object of knowledge, an object of the intellect. It is the unfathomable openness of absolute reality, shining radiantly.

Even a great metropolis like New York, which so many people worked so hard to put together, looks like a permanent meeting of people. In a few hundred years, who knows what it will look like, or if it will even be there? And even if there are still many people and cars there, they will certainly not be the same people and cars. Everything is impermanent in this world, including one's own body, one's own fleeting illusory body, a temporary compounded phenomenon, the mere result of the joining of the male and female essences through one's karmic father and mother in this life. But in one hundred years, where will this body be?

Everything is like that. This is neither something to frighten or appall or depress us, nor is it said in order to belittle our importance. This is just the nature of compounded phenomena. We will all die and decompose, leaving everything behind, except our karmic accumulations. And at that time, when we go forth from this life, only our merits and realization are of benefit to us. Nothing else of this present body and life remains.

This is not praise, and this is not blame, neither pessimism nor optimism; there is no judgment here. This is simply an objective recognition of how things truly are, which we ourselves could also recognize and realize: that all compounded phenomena are fleeting, illusory, unstable and impermanent. All compounded phenomena come into being through the law of interdependent origination. They are all interconnected, interdependent. When the causes and conditions come together, things momentarily appear. When the causes and conditions are exhausted, things fall apart, as when a fire burns itself out when the fuel is exhausted. This is how relative phenomena come into being in the context of the great emptiness. There is no creator other than the impersonal law of causation, karmic cause and effect. Those who know these two truths, the relative interdependence and the absolute emptiness, are called the fearless heroes, the courageous bodhisattvas, the awakening spiritual warriors.

That is why in our lineage, since the time of Longchenpa's great disciple Vidyadhara Jigme Lingpa in the eighteenth century, all the masters, from Jigme Lingpa to Gyalwai Nyugu to Patrul Rinpoche and down through today, were given the first name Jigme, meaning fearless. They recognize the unchanging absolute emptiness, the essential nature of their own minds. Amidst the very transient, dreamlike, and illusory relative phenomena, they are fearless in the face of death and impermanence.

Ordinary beings do not often explicitly acknowledge, in the forefront of their consciousness, their undeniable fear of death, illness, old age, loneliness, painful questions and difficulties of all kinds; for example, fear of losing what they have, of experiencing what they don't want to experience, of getting what they don't want, of not getting what they do want, and so on. Therefore, their whole being is entangled in anxiety, hope, and fear—the endless proliferation of attachments and fixations. Hope and fear is a huge limitation, spawning infinite complications.

How can we actualize the impeccable fearless courage of the awakened warriors, the heroic bodhisattvas? The true nature or condition of all things is the great shunyata, which is not just a vacuum, a void, an empty; but it is luminous emptiness. It has a quality of "isness," of suchness, the *tathagatagarbha*. It is the emptiness endowed with the heart of compassion or wisdom. It is called the natural Great Perfection, the innate Great Perfection, Dzogpa Chenpo; this great emptiness endowed with the core of luminosity, the inseparability of cognizance and emptiness, of awareness and compassion. Where truth and unconditional love are not different.

The fundamental ground, or basis, of the ultimate nature of being, is called the ground Dzogpa Chenpo—the fundamental innate Great Perfection. It is pure, perfect, and complete from the beginningless beginning, lacking nothing, free from alteration or change. It is neither improved in nirvana nor ruined in samsara. It remains adamantine, transcendent, untrammeled by causes and conditions: the natural Great Perfection. *Emaho!*

Although this luminous Great Perfection, Dzogpa Chenpo, is one without a second, one indivisible homogenous whole, for the sake of explication it is subdivided into ground, path, and fruition. Dzogchen is explained in terms of these three, which are actually indivisible, too, yet are explicated as a triad for the sake of clarity: view, meditation, and action.

View means outlook, perspective, overview; *meditation* refers to the actual practice of getting used to that view, which one has been introduced to, and which one has identified or confirmed experientially for oneself; and the *action*, or behavior, is the actual enlightened activity in life. Although the fundamental basis or ground is one, whole, and inseparable, these three can be elucidated as proceeding from one to another: first, there must be the view, then true meditation and action proceed, one after another, from that awareness and recognition. Although in absolute truth, the fundamental ground and fruit are inseparable, in relative reality the path must still be traversed to complete that rainbow-like bridge.

Inherent in this great emptiness—this openness and luminosity, the true nature of one's mind, the innate Great Perfection—are inconceivable qualities, all of the enlightened qualities of the Buddhas of all directions, of the past, present, and future. These transcendental qualities are inherently present. We could say that they are potential, but it is not a potential that has to be developed in the future. They are inherently present, and accessible even today.

If and when a practitioner recognizes the true nature of his or her own innate being, the ultimate nature of mind, the natural Great Perfection, then, in one lifetime, in this very body—in even a very few years, or even mere mind-moments—perfect supreme Buddhahood is actualized.

This innate Great Perfection, this basic goodness called buddha-nature, buddha-mind, or *rigpa*, is our own nature. It is our very own "stream of being," *gyu*, in Tibetan. It is our very own being. It is not just our mind. It is our being. It is what we are. That is why it is called the swift and cozy, or comfy, path. It doesn't require a lot of effort, hardship, or austerities, or extensive duration of practice, like when it says that the Bodhisattvayana takes three endless eons to be accomplished. It is in this life, it is in this moment: right now, the instantaneous moment of Dzogchen, called rigpa recognition. *Emaho!*

All-knowing Longchenpa said,

> Since things are beyond good and bad,
> Attachment and aversion, adopting and abandoning,
> When I see how caught up beings are in this illusory magical
>   display,
> How can I not burst out laughing!

In the general teachings of Buddhism, in the sutras and general practice vehicles, it takes many lifetimes to develop through the stages (*bhumis*) and realize Buddhahood or the other fruits of the path. In the Dzogchen teaching, the swift and comfy path is right now. When the moment of Dzogchen has arrived, in the very moment of recognizing it, of getting used to it, of ascertaining total inner conviction, that is the crucial moment, the great moment of Dzogchen. It is not something in the future. That is why it is called the swift, naked, direct path, the vajra shortcut, the dawn of Vajrasattva, adamantine being.

This really is right now, ever-present, ever-accessible. That is why we exclaim, *Emaho!* and call it the wondrous, joyous Dharma of Dzogchen. It is marvelous, fantastic, far out, incredible—however you choose to translate that great joy. It is a shortcut. It is the direct path. It is a way of unsheathing our buddha-nature from the scabbard of concepts, of duality. The sword of rigpa is there always. Why not unsheathe it, and brandish it fearlessly in the unobstructed sky?

When one has the auspicious or appropriate karmic connection to the teacher and the teachings, faith, trust, and devotion arise for the teacher and the teachings, and one is in the right place at the right time. When all these conditions are fulfilled, there is nothing to obstruct the direct, naked experience of one's intrinsic awareness, the true nature of one's mind, the innate Great Perfection. This innate perfection and completeness of our own being is what these teachings point directly to, not some sort of mystic treasure in far-off Tibet. There is no need to be anxiously looking everywhere, writing down every tidbit of information about this experience and visiting every lama in the world. One can really experience right here and now one's own true nature, rigpa, this ineffable primordial presence. Even right now it is available and welcoming—this open, expansive, and un-self-preoccupied mind.

When you listen to such teachings as these, the words are just like little bubbles or sparks popping into the air and dissolving. If you write them down in a notebook and put the notebook on a shelf, after some months they just gather a lot of dust, and they will become something outside of oneself that one doesn't have time for and one wishes to get and find time for, to somehow retrieve into oneself. This can be just another cause of stress. However, the true meaning of these words is what is in ourselves even now. It doesn't have to be written down and put on the bookshelf. It can never gather dust. We always have time to access it, to relate to it. If we don't relate to it right now, when will we?

In the general teachings of the various vehicles there is quite a bit to read and learn, like the *Tripitaka*, with all of its divisions, and the sutras and tantras too. But this teaching—the direct, naked path of the intrinsic awareness called Dzogchen—is beyond the mind. It is the moment for all dualistic perceptions to fall apart, or to be left in their natural state, in their own way, which is the vast openness and emptiness of shunyata. This is the outlook, the view. This is also the practice and the enlightened way to live our daily life. So, this encompasses the view, meditation, and action of Dzogchen. There is nothing very much to do except to rest in that which one has recognized, or been introduced to, has discovered for oneself, within oneself—the innate Great Perfection, pure and authentic presence.

The great, glorious enlightened vagabond, Patrul Rinpoche, said that in the general paths—referring to most Buddhist vehicles—it is like chaining one thought to another, an endless chain of discursiveness that we get tangled in, due to our own willful efforts. But in the path of Dzogchen, all appearances, all phenomena, spontaneously dissolve in their own natural state, self-appearing, self-releasing, beyond fixation and reference point. There is simply nothing to bind or entangle, and no one to be entangled. Everything is left just as it is, in its natural way, however it appears. In the Trekchod or Cutting Through teachings of the natural Great Perfection, Longchenpa sang, "Leave it as it is, and rest your weary mind." For there is really nothing to be lost or gained, nothing to hope for or be afraid of.

Allow the mind to go wherever it will, as the *Diamond Sutra* suggests when it states, "Cultivate the awareness that abides nowhere." The Mahamudra master, the Indian siddha Maitripa, sang, "Let thoughts go free, just like a dove released from a ship in the middle of the infinite ocean. For just as the bird finds nowhere to land but back on the ship, thoughts have no place to go other than returning to their place of origin." Know this source, mind-essence itself, and be free.

Who knows the true nature of things? The actual knower—the empty, cognizant aspect of mind—is the primordial Buddha, Samantabhadra, the personification of one's own rigpa. Rigpa, the primordial Buddha Samantabhadra, is very, very important. It is the clear light, luminous buddha-nature, that which *knows*. Innate awareness-wisdom, rigpa, is functioning through us even now, if we only knew it.

The worldly minds of beings, endowed with the same cognizance or knowingness, use awareness to not know, to delude themselves. It is very important to know that this is how it occurs; not just to know the primordial Buddha, but to know the primordial ignorance of beings, how it actually operates.

Within that state of primordial awareness, or gnosis, rests Samantabhadra, "All-Good," meaning everything is good, everything is perfect from the beginningless beginning. Whatever arises, Samantabhadra recognizes as self-radiance, spontaneous display, not as separate dualistic perceptions; thus Samantabhadra remains free from the beginning within that expanse of all things recognized and appreciated as creative, spontaneous display. When things arise in the minds of beings, however, they are misperceived as different, as "other," as duality. In this confusion, beings become alienated, confused (like Narcissus), and through their own ignorance get lost in self-deception and all kinds of difficulties and suffering.

That is why it says in Samantabhadra's Aspiration Prayer (which is not a prayer to Samantabhadra, but is Samantabhadra's own prayerful affirmation), "One ground, two paths." It means that there is one single ground of being, of both the primordial Buddha and deluded beings; yet there are two possible paths: the path of primordial perfection, and the path of delusion and bondage.

All beings, knowingly or unknowingly, want and need to encounter this immanent primordial perfection, so-called Samantabhadra. But how to encounter or meet that Buddha which is their very own nature? This is the point of the path, the practice path of Dzogchen. It is difficult to meet that primordial Buddha, the dharmakaya Buddha, Samantabhadra. Therefore, on the energy level the *dharmakaya* manifests as the *sambhogakaya*, Dorje Chang, Vajradhara; or even in this world, in the *nirmanakaya*, as Shakyamuni, teaching in words and in form. Beings can actually meet this reality in person in a way they can appreciate.

These three Buddhas—primordial Buddha Samantabhadra, which is total dharmakaya, absolute formless reality; sambhogakaya, Vajradhara or Dorje Chang, which is the energy level, visionary level; and nirmanakaya, the form body, Shakyamuni, the historical Buddha—these three Buddhas are actually one personification of rigpa. Those who have incredibly good karma, accumulations of merit and wisdom, can have the good fortune to meet in person the bodily form of Buddha Shakyamuni; for example, those who lived in India at Buddha's time. This is a coincidence or a coming together of their excellent karma with the Buddha's five hundred great prayers, over five hundred Bodhisattva lifetimes, to be able to benefit beings after reaching perfect enlightenment. Thus, the coming together of his prayers, and the good karma, the positive actions of certain beings, brought certain people together in this very world at the time of the Buddha. That is not an opportunity that many of us have, to meet Shakyamuni Buddha in person. Yet we have the good fortune to meet his living representatives in person: the enlightened teachers in the various traditions and lineages stemming from him.

The teaching of Dzogchen, Dzogpa Chenpo, is sometimes called Maha Ati, because it belongs to the ninth class of tantra, Maha Ati Yoga Tantra. "Ati" means summit or peak, because with the view from above, from the very top of the mountain, you can see all the sides of the mountain and all the paths leading up from below. You have the overview, the bigger picture. While some people seem to be ascending the spiritual mountain in one way, perhaps winding upwards in a clockwise direction, others are coming up by a counter-clockwise route; if you see from above, you can see all the different paths ascending the same mountain. But when you look from below, it can seem that people are going in different directions, on different paths, and it can seem contradictory and irreconcilable. In fact, all the paths are converging on the great summit of the ultimate evolution of being, Buddhahood, the Great Perfection.

When we have the view from above, we see how all paths and practices fit together, what their core or guiding principle is. However, from below it is often as if we cannot see the forest because we are lost in the trees. Therefore, it is important to be introduced to the view from above—even while we are practicing the relative practices from below—as a guiding principle, so that our relative practices are greatly enhanced by the view of absolute reality, and we have an authentic overview, even as we work gradually through various stages.

We should not get involved in sectarianism or criticism. Sometimes, in different Buddhist countries or different teachings, people say, "Oh, those deities the lama described, like Vajradhara, that has nothing to do with Buddha. That's some other kind of teaching. It's mixed with Hinduism." Or perhaps, "Those deities are just like Hindu deities. That's not pure Buddhism. Buddhism doesn't have deities. Buddhism is non-theistic, relies only on buddha-nature." Or, "Only Tibetan Buddhism can bring authentic enlightenment in one lifetime." This is confusion, a partial bias, the view from below; we cannot see the whole forest because of the multitude of trees. But when we practice according to Dzogchen, it is as if we climb up from below (through relative means), while understanding the view from above (absolute reality), using these two wings (relative and absolute truth) to wing our way directly to Buddhahood.

We can look at it like this: We ascend from below through spirituality, with practice—the relative practices, including our behavior, ethics, and meditation; while at the same time we descend from above with the vast view. In that way the relative and absolute are coincident, joined, in whatever practices we do. This is the practice of the six perfections, each one totally imbued with *prajnaparamita*, the sixth perfection. And this is the way, the practice, of the Great Perfection in the context of the Bodhisattva Vehicle: descending from above with the view—understanding according to the ultimate view, absolute truth, shunyata; while ascending from below through relative practices, according to our actual capacity.

One day a yogi descended from his cave to beg for alms, and he met a gathering of children in the marketplace. They were fighting among each other, quarreling and squabbling. One said, "My father has the most beautiful golden face and complexion, and is bigger than anyone else's father." Another boy said, "My uncle has the most fantastic shining face. It's like a lotus. He's stronger than anybody else's uncle." And somebody else said, "No, it's my father who's the most beautiful and handsome and strongest." And somebody else said, "No, it's my uncle who's the most loving and magnificent and powerful." Each little boy had their own principal father figure, and they were all fighting over who was the best. They were fighting so much that the yogi couldn't even explain anything to them. He just went back to his cave and wrote this story, connecting it to the sectarian strife of his own day.

Isn't this very much like the sectarianism among different religious schools, not only within Buddhism but in all the religions? Each boy has his own father or uncle, which is natural, and he thinks that they are the best, which they are for him. Nor is there anyone who needs to adjudicate and decide who is the best father or guardian. Each child has a parent, which is sufficient. Similarly, just like all of the schools of Buddhism, we too follow Lord Buddha. And yet we find ourselves squabbling about which Buddha is best, Buddha Shakyamuni, or the primordial Buddha Samantabhadra, or the Buddha Vajradhara, or other Buddhas—deities, for example, like Chenrezig, Tara, Amitabha, or Manjushri. However we dress him or her up, whoever the parent figure is, we are fighting as if we are all of different tribes, and it is our job to find out who is the best. It is just like those children, each loving their own parent and promoting him or her as best. It is childish.

When we realize the ultimate nature of Dzogchen, we actualize awakened buddhahood. Then there is nothing else to do. There is really no discussion needed about which is the best way to get there. The ultimate nature of all things, this mahashunyata endowed with the luminous heart of compassion, is personified as the primordial Buddha Samantabhadra, the very personification of one's own innate awareness, rigpa. It is the tathagatagarbha, the buddha-nature in all beings. It is what the Buddha Shakyamuni realized under the bodhi tree in Bodhgaya when the morning star dawned on the eastern horizon. What he awoke to, experienced within himself, is the very nature of all sentient beings, without exception. It is what the master, the omniscient Dzogchen master Longchenpa, realized in his own body-mind continuum. That is why he is called *Long-chen*, the great expanse, referring to the infinite empty expanse, the infinity of one's own empty nature.

All of these things are synonymous when seen as they are. The name of the Dzogchen master Longchen Rabjam means infinite great expanse. It is synonymous with mahashunyata endowed with the heart of great compassion. It is a lama's name, but we don't worship a particular person or lama. We affirm and actualize the meaning of that name, that one's own nature is the infinite great expanse. There are so many spiritual masters who have recognized this true intrinsic nature, this inexpressible so-called reality, this infinite vast expanse, not only Longchen Rabjam. Actually, all of these realized masters are inseparable in the buddha-mind, rigpa, which is what has realized it as well as what is realized.

Even in this world, and even now, there are said to be many hidden yogis or discreet yogis, called *bepay naljor* in Tibetan. It means those realized ones who are not generally recognized as great spiritual sages or saints, but have deeply tasted the fruit of enlightenment, and are living it. Perhaps they are anonymously doing their good works here among us right now!

This infinite vast expanse is one's own inconceivable nature. Who can say who has realized it and who hasn't? When we travel around the world or experience other dimensions, there are so many beings who have tasted it. We can see it in their behavior, in their countenance, and in stories that are told—not just in the Dzogchen tradition or the Buddhist tradition, but in any tradition, and in our Western world too.

This true nature is so vast and inconceivable that even some birds and animals and beings in other unseen dimensions can be said to have realized it, as in some of the ancient Indian *Jataka* stories and other teaching tales. It is always said that everything is the self-radiant display of the primordial Buddha Samantabhadra. There are infinite numbers of Buddhas and infinite numbers of beings. Who can say who is excluded from it?

In the Dzogchen tantras, this infinite primordial purity (*kadak*) is clearly explained, including all things and all beings. According to the tantras, it is very important to cultivate and practice this kind of sacred outlook, pure vision: recognizing everything as perfect by nature, not seeing some beings as lower and deluded, and some beings as higher, more evolved, enlightened; perceiving all beings as part of that boundless mandala of the innate Great Perfection.

If you meet a teacher who represents the lineage and tradition of Dzogchen, this is also a partial idea; it is good fortune, but it is still a limited notion. There is no real need to take too seriously the idea that one lama represents Dzogchen or Mahamudra, and everywhere else are teachers and people who do not, as other beings have nothing to do with Dzogchen. Authentic sacred vision, the pure perception often mentioned in the tantric path, implies that we can and should see everything as perfectly pure and inherently good; that is, beyond good and bad, perfectly complete just as it is, however it momentarily manifests; because, free from clinging to duality, everything is merely a display of the dharmata, absolute reality, suchness. It is the self-display or self-radiance of rigpa, of Samantabhadra Buddha. It is the echo-like self-resounding of the dharmata, the absolute state of all things. We are all inseparable from that.

The true Dzogchen yogis have an open, accommodating heart and mind, excluding nothing from their perfect mandala of pure perception. Brimming over with wisdom, unconditional love, and empathy, they do not need to adopt any particular way of looking or acting, they do not need to abandon and reject anything either.

This is called the spontaneous activity, or carefree ease, of Dzogpa Chenpo. It is not something we can easily imitate. Yet to whatever extent we can recognize and participate in it, great benefit ensues, for oneself and others.

In the beginning of a vajra song I sang, "Praise to my twenty-five spiritual masters." I had twenty-five gracious root gurus as well as many other teachers, beginning with the renowned Khenpo Ngakga, Patrul Rinpoche's grand-disciple, and Khenpo Ngakga's disciple, Nyoshul Shedrup Tenpai Nyima, my own personal root guru and mentor. These lamas embodied to me all the excellent awakened qualities spoken of in the sutras, tantras, and *shastras*.

To begin this song about great emptiness, I sang, "Homage to the great master Longchen Rabjam, inseparable from my own root gurus, those who recognize the infinite vast expanse of intrinsic awareness, particularly Shedrup Tenpai Nyima, the sun and moon of learning and spiritual accomplishment. To them I pay homage and prostrate. At their lotus feet I pay homage and prostrate."

I feel infinite gratitude, veneration, and appreciation to those glorious vajra masters, the lineage masters and my own root gurus, who gave me everything: not just spiritual teaching and personal guidance, but even food, clothes, and protection in my youth. I can never quite repay the gratitude that I owe to them.

Gratitude to the teachers and the lineage and root gurus actually stretches back to the Buddha Shakyamuni himself, who so compassionately appeared in this very world to teach and liberate us. Lord Buddha is the teacher of all the teachers. All positive qualities that have arisen in the lineage are due to his kindness and his teachings, the sublime Buddhadharma.

The first gratitude and homage is to ones called "those above." This refers to those of the past or those higher, more evolved beings, such as the lineage of root masters and Buddhas. The second gratitude is to those who are equal to us, particularly the most important, one's own dear mother of this life, who gave birth to this precious human life, this body, with all its leisures, opportunities, endowments, and possibilities, including encountering and practicing the liberation path called Buddhadharma.

All praise, homage, and gratitude to my own mother, Chodzom Palsang, who gave me life, who gave me my body, who nurtured me day and night when I was a helpless infant, who brought me up, was my first teacher, and taught me the ways of the world, including how to do the smallest things without which I couldn't today be alive. My own mother gave birth to this human body endowed with the eight freedoms and the ten endowments. One can read what these are in the different Lam Rim texts, explaining the preliminary practices.

I wrote *The Mirror of Essential Points* when I was in Dordogne, after being in France for five or six years, to tell my devoted mother what was happening to her little wandering child, who had come to foreign lands where people fly in the sky in silver birds and travel under the earth and under the sea in powerful machines; where there are so many different colors and experiences of all kinds; where there are all kinds of men and women of different colors, big and small, where some wear hundreds of clothes as adornments on their body, and others have the scantiest of clothes, or walk nude at the seaside; while I myself wander around with nothing but old orange wraps and a straw hat to shield my bald wrinkled head from the sun; where there are machines hundreds of trees high, buildings which reach down hundreds of meters below the earth, and people travel in fast trains, supersonic airplanes, in nuclear submarines; where scientists seem to have control over even the sunrise and moonrise, and can play with the five elements—air, water, fire, wind, and ether or space—like gods, like magicians, flying to the moon, and heading even towards the sun; where there are people who are rich beyond belief, and people who are poor beyond assistance; people who have so many different dreamlike experiences, the likes of which one has never heard of, dreamed of, nor would be likely to believe in Tibet; and who seem to be lost in the darkness of delusion, just like so many in Tibet and India, with or without material benefits—still thirsting for peace, contentment, and fulfillment, lacking spiritual peace and realization.

I have seen so many different kinds of displays that one could never possibly describe them all. But if you see this clearly and have a good look at it, all these incredible, miraculous displays are just the dreamlike display of one's own mind. It is just a matter of one's perception, how one experiences things, just as a glass of water might seem very different to a small fish, who could live in it as a home, than to we humans.

No matter how amazing it is, when one recognizes everything as the display or projection of one's own mind, when we see that all perceptions depend on one's own karma, then one is no longer amazed, because one understands how things actually work, and how they are, and we can live harmoniously, and appreciate everything just as it is. There are so many things to see. But what are they really? It is like a dream, a mirage, an illusion, a magician's hallucination. Some dreams last a hundred years and then dissolve. Some dreams last one minute or one hour and then dissolve. Others take concrete form and seem to last longer before dispersing.

Everything is ultimately resolved in the absolute nature. Within such dreamlike phenomena, what is there to adopt or cling to? What is there to judge? What is there to reject or abandon? There is nothing to either pick up or put down. When you awaken—when you recognize the dreamlike nature of appearances—what is there to do? It is just a dream—so what? There is nothing more to do about it, other than to know the dreamer, the knower. Who is dreaming, anyway?

Mahasiddha Saraha sang, "In the ten directions, what is there to fabricate or look for or do? Recognize the insubstantiality and unreality of all apparent phenomena." Everything is free, just as it is. What to do about it?

Outside it is like that; inside oneself it is like that, too. Inside there is an unceasing, movie-like display of *namtok*, discursive thoughts and concepts, isn't there? Internally, what is the basis for the display of *noumena*, mental phenomena, namtok? Where do they come from? Where do they abide temporarily, and where do they go or dissolve? What are they? What is thinking, or concept? Examine that internally, observe the mind, just as one has examined externally the endless magical display, the dreamlike illusory spectacle of this fleeting world.

All thoughts, feelings, emotions, perceptions, sensations, states of mind, concepts, and so on are like clouds in the sky, momentarily coming together and then dispersing, dissolving back in that very same space. What good can it do to cling to them? What good can it do to try to drive them away? Everything is the illusory, miraculous dreamlike display of one's own mind. There is nothing special to do about that, except to recognize its true, empty nature, and be free within whatever seems to appear. It is not necessary to judge thoughts and experiences as good or bad, as desirable or undesirable, profitable or unprofitable. Let them come and go just as they are, without becoming overly involved, without identifying with anything, neither indulging in them by following after them nor suppressing or inhibiting them. Simply let all inner and outer things appear and disappear in their own way, just like clouds in the sky, and remain above and beyond it all, even amidst one's daily activities and responsibilities.

There are so many things to do in this world, but there is only one thing that one needs to know, and that is one's true nature. That is the universal medicine, the panacea that cures all ills and disease. Whatever comes, also goes. One's nature, one's true fundamental being, is beyond or unaffected by all adventitious stains or temporary phenomena. It does not come and go; it remains immutable. Recognizing that, innate transcendence is experienced. Then samsara and nirvana present neither hope nor fear for the practitioner; duality has ceased to obtain. There is nothing to look forward to, nothing to fall back into.

As Guru Rinpoche has said, as Tilopa and Naropa said, as the Mahasiddha Saraha said, "With outer objects be unconcerned. With inner objects (the subject itself) be unconcerned. Without looking without or within, leave it as it is—empty, free, and open. It is not outer objects that bind us, but internal clinging that entangles us."

This is the essential pith-instruction of the mahasiddhas of India and the accomplished yogis of Tibet. It is based on the words of the Buddha Shakyamuni himself, who said that the root of all suffering is clinging, attachment. There is no teaching other than this. This is the root of all. This is the principle behind all the many different explanations.

Sensuality is not in objects, it is in the desiring mind, in desire itself. Desire invests objects with desirability, sensuality, and value. Otherwise, what is ultimately desirable? Everything depends on the mind, on one's conditioning; what one person desires and longs for another might abhor and avoid at all cost. Isn't that obvious?

Therefore, whatever teaching one has received, rest in great evenness, emptiness, and lucid openness, beyond clinging and fixation. This is the threshold of experiencing the true nature of the innate

Great Perfection, Mahashunyata: beyond all concepts and efforts, opening to the effortlessness of true freedom and authentic, untrammeled being.

Some might misunderstand and wonder: Then why bother with virtuous actions and accumulating merits or helping others? Why generate loving-kindness and compassion? Others might think: Why not continue to perform negative actions, since in emptiness everything is equal? This is a grave misunderstanding. This is a danger, a deviation from the view. This is nihilism, where the yawning abyss of pseudo-emptiness beckons.

When one realizes the natural state, the true nature of all beings, there is naturally a welling up of inconceivable spontaneous compassion, loving-kindness, consideration, and empathy, because one realizes there is no self separate from others. One then treats others just like oneself. There is no cause for aversion, attachment, or exploitation. Authentic spiritual realization is naturally endowed with inconceivable qualities such as compassion, loving-kindness, and helpfulness. Everyone is seen as just like oneself, not a permanent independent entity but an interdependent, karmically conditioned temporary conglomeration of forces. So one alleviates suffering and distress wherever it appears, within or without, whether for oneself or others. Why wouldn't you? No one wants suffering, right?

When you realize the true nature of things, how can you not have incredible spontaneous compassion for all those who don't realize it? Beings all want happiness, yet, due to ignorance, continually create further suffering for themselves. What a cause for compassion! Beings mistake that which is illusory, unreal, and impermanent for that which is real and permanent. What a cause for compassion! Beings see that which is beneficial as useless, and ignore it. What a cause for compassion! Everywhere that suffering and delusion arise, compassion arises to release and alleviate beings suffering from that delusion. That is the spontaneous outflow of the genuine realization of the true nature.

It is just like when one sees children running out in the street, and one naturally reaches out to save them from traffic. It is not a question of thinking about it. It is not a question of whose children they are. One just naturally responds. This is called compassion, but it is not really conceptualized compassion. It is just appropriate action, basic sanity. This is the spontaneous enlightened behavior, the natural compassion, that is the result of true realization.

It is said in these pith-instructions that when one recognizes the true nature, or perceives one's original face, even a dog-faced person, even a lion-faced person, becomes Buddha in this very lifetime. Even an illiterate person, even a learned person, becomes Buddha in this very lifetime. This means that there are no particular prerequisites for realization, only a total breakthrough, which does not necessarily depend on learning, piety, status, or prestige.

Please don't think that we are here in this world for a very long time. This is a very short meeting. And yet, this is the moment of Dzogchen; it is beyond duration, beyond time and space. We have the fortunate connection to make contact with a teaching and an opportunity to practice. It is not just that the seed has been planted, because one can actually experience the fruit right now. If one really matures or deepens in practice, this is the moment; it is not in the future. Don't think one needs more time. It is a matter of practice now.

To reflect on the teachings does not necessarily mean that you have to study every audiotape and book that has accumulated. Simply reflect on whatever has stayed in mind from these teachings, even if it's the smallest single theme or word, such as impermanence, or insubstantiality, or dreamlike. Because the time of practice is not the time to waste time and play around. One can also play around intellectually with studies and debates and books, which can provide great pleasure, but are a distraction too, just more sophisticated forms of playing around.

Everybody likes to fool around and enjoy themselves. I myself love to study the hundreds of thousands of glorious *shlokas* of Dzogchen teachings. However, listening to tapes is not really the ultimate way to realize Dzogchen. Sometimes a lot of study only increases discursivity and gives rise to more doubts and complicated questions. Then we have more intellectual investigations to make, while right now we could resolve all those possible doubts and issues through simple practice.

When we know how to really practice and meditate, there is no need to keep looking for other ways to do it and other teachings about it. It is very delightful to have many different kinds of teachings, but if we would really sever the root of duality, we need to apply ourselves in practice right now, not sometime in the future, after having collected all the possible teachings on the subject.

I have tried very hard throughout my entire life to receive all the transmissions and teachings from twenty-five enlightened Tibetan masters of different lineages. But in fact, all we need to know is how to meditate and put these things in practice.

If these few words of heartfelt advice can benefit and prove useful to you, then all of my efforts throughout my whole life have been meaningful. Some individuals might think that Dzogchen is just another strange foreign cult or trip. If there is a great deal of debate, comparative religion, philosophical hair-splitting, and comparisons, perhaps my efforts have been in vain.

I hope you understand what I am trying to say. Practice well, and take advantage of these moments and these teachings. The root is to have confidence in the three jewels: the outer, inner, and secret levels of understanding Buddha, Dharma, and Sangha. Devotion and compassion can also be extremely helpful, for they unsheathe the freshness of awareness itself, and enhance the luster of rigpa. Do not overlook the supportive nature of relative practices. Use whatever is meaningful and workable for you.

There is no one else who can do your practice for you. It must be suitable for you yourself, not a mere imitation of someone else's practice, however good it may appear on the surface. Please clarify things for yourself, as much as you possibly can. Then everything will be perfectly fulfilled.

Sarva mangalam. May all things be auspicious!

8 The Vajra Mirror of Mindfulness

A Spontaneous Song
Dordogne, France 1982

Translated by Padmakara Translation Group

Homage to the sovereign king within: self-arising mindfulness.
I am the vajra of mindfulness.
Look, vajra friends! When seeing me, be mindful.
I am the mirror of mindfulness,
I mirror your careful attention.
Look clearly, moment by moment, and see directly into the very
  essence of mind.

Mindfulness is the root of Dharma.
Mindfulness is the body of practice.
Mindfulness is the fortress of the mind.
Mindfulness is the aid to the wisdom of innate wakefulness.
Mindfulness is the support of Mahamudra, Maha Ati, Dzogchen,
  and Madhyamika.

Lack of mindfulness will allow the negative forces to overcome
  you.
Without mindfulness you will be swept away by laziness.
Lack of mindfulness is the creator of evil deeds.
Without mindfulness and presence of mind, nothing can be
  accomplished.

Lack of mindfulness piles up lots of shit.
Without mindfulness you sleep in an ocean of piss.

Without mindfulness you are a heartless zombie, a walking corpse.
Dear Dharma friends, please be mindful!
By the aspiration of the holy lamas, Buddhas, bodhisattvas, and
   lineage masters,
May all vajra friends attain stable mindfulness and ascend the
   throne of perfect awakening!

*These few words were extemporaneously composed by the buck-
toothed foolish ox, the fallen monk, Jamyang Dorje, and offered to
his vajra friends, who are endowed with the eyes of Dharma.*
   Virtue, happiness and peace! Sarva mangalam!

9 Deer Park Retreat

Dai Bosatsu Zendo
Livingston Manor, New York, 1992

Translated by David Christensen

Homage to the primordial Buddha, Samantabhadra!

Not recognizing the Victors' realm, innate immaculate *dharmakaya,*
Beings wander in this conditioned world,
Stranded in the very midst of this vast plain of sorrow, karma and
    kleshas.
Far better to rest your weary mind.

Kye Ho! O, my extremely fortunate friends,
Here in this supreme place of the ultimate, vast sky-like expanse—
    longchen rabjam,
Look at this wonderfully pure sight.

Externally: Unfabricated, this natural forest,
Adorned with thousands of variegated colors,
Trees, creepers, leaves, flowers,
All kinds of birds, deer, skunks, turkeys, and other wild animals
    frolicking,
While delightfully resounds the melodious humming of all types
    of creatures,
And a shower of snowflakes wafts down from the sky,
Shaped like flowers, petals, and divine objects.

In this place, totally free of the cacophony of meaningless worldly
    babble,
Which would disturb the practice of meditative serenity,
Within this naturally tranquil forest
Is the supreme place for accomplishing wisdom and *samadhi*.
Emaho, how wonderful!

Internally: Unfabricated, intrinsic nature of mind is dharmakaya,
Naturally arising, naturally liberating,
Natural clarity unimpeded.
The innate wisdom-mind expanse of Samantabhadra
Is beyond all causes and conditions,
All objects, fixations, efforts, and fabrications.

Free of all limitations and partiality, the primordial Buddha,
One's own mind, Samantabhadra.
Don't seek elsewhere, outside oneself, for the ultimate sovereign:
Rigpa, supreme wisdom of intrinsic awareness,
Natural sky-like wisdom-mind.
Emaho!

In between: Unfabricated, one's body is a buddha-field.
Aggregates, constituents, and sense fields
Are primordially pure and perfect,
Uncreated by anyone, the innate deity *mandala*.
The five sense objects and phenomena of six consciousnesses:
Whatever arises simply displays the wisdom of bliss inseparable
    from emptiness.

By the esoteric path of innate Great Perfection, Dzogchen,
Vajra songs and dances and all sorts of creative joys burst forth,
An ocean-like feast-offering of boundless delights.
Samsara and nirvana are equally enjoyed, in one taste, as the
    experience of great bliss.

All the various phenomena, however they appear,
Have never wavered, even slightly, from the *dharmadhatu*.
Within the vast expanse (*longchen*) of dharmakaya, Samanta-
    bhadra's wisdom-mind,

All the infinite (*rabjam*) multifarious appearances, however they
  arise,
Are perfect and complete within the recognition of natural
  equality,
The innate natural Great Perfection beyond the intellect,
The noble *longchen rabjam*, great infinite expanse.
Emaho!

Hundreds of thousands of immaculate light rays (*drimé oser*) of
  the sun
Naturally purify the great ignorance, the heart's darkness.
Samsara all perfect (*kunzang*), nirvana all perfect (*kunzang*),
Self-arisen, innate *vajra*, fearless master Jigme Lingpa,
May we assume spiritual sovereignty in the immutable
  dharmakaya!

*This was written by the wandering khenpo of Nyoshul, Jamyang
Dorje, a stray dog from the snow land of Tibet, at the two-month
Dzogchen mountain retreat in the United States, led by the Dzog-
chen yogi Lama Surya Das, together with many Western Dharma
teachers and spiritual friends.*
  May it be virtuous!

10 The Song of Illusion:
Khenpo Jamyang Dorje's Letter
of Instructions to His Disciples
Dordogne, France 1981

Translated by Padmakara Translation Group

Homage to the Guru!
Illusory wisdom reflection of Drimé Oser,
Inseparable from Jampel Pawo, only father of all the Buddhas,
Who manifested in this decadent age to guide beings to liberation,
O, my root teacher, Tenpai Nyima, you know all things!
Self-arisen Dharma lord, show the undeluded nature of the mind
To those who through delusion are deceived by false appearances.

Kye Ho! Listen carefully, fortunate friends,
Swans dwelling on the glorious summer lake of the Buddha's
    doctrine!
To my disciples and *vajra* brothers and sisters long known to me,
I offer a spontaneous letter to tell you how I am, a song of illusion.
Do not think it is wrong of me to express myself openly,
But listen well to it, the playful friend of your golden lotus ears.

Although in this life I possess no great qualities,
Through the perfect merit of pure actions previously accumulated,
I met the incomparable lama, jewel of the sky.
With faith like a lake of stainless milk, white on the surface and
    below,

I exerted myself in serving my spiritual friend, the root of all
Dharma.
And just as, at the foot of a mountain of precious gold,
Even ordinary pebbles are tinted with its radiance,
So too my mind—trapped in the net of discursive thoughts,
fettered by common delusion,
The spiked iron chains of intense duality and clinging to
solidity—found rest.
A beggar, free from activity, relaxed in a happy, open state of mind,
I destroyed the web of the eight worldly concerns of illusory hopes
and fears.

The king of Dharma, Longchen Rabjam, said,
"Activities are endless, like ripples on a stream,
They end when we leave them: such is their nature."
So too, through the kindness of the lama who taught me
non-activity and self-appearance,
The thought arose in me that without doing anything, everything
is accomplished.

In front there is no one I need to protect: a *yogin*, I am happy!
Behind, no one to sustain: alone, I am joyful!
I have no work to put off: with no time lost, I am happy!
I have no use for long-term plans: relaxed, I am joyful!
Criticized, I am not depressed: undismayed, I am happy!

Through the kindness of the lama who showed me the great middle
path,
As Buddha taught, not swayed by either extreme of life's
necessities,
Though I sleep in a lovely mansion of the finest gold,
Overflowing with heaps of various jewels,
I have no need to be haughty or seek admiration.
Though I dwell in cool shady gardens of fruit trees, the excellent
refuge of the lower man,
Or huts of latticed grass,
I have no need for lament. My mind is not seized by hopes and
fears.
Through the kindness of the teacher who taught me the
pre-eminence of the supreme *bodhi*-mind,

I remain loving and kind to whoever I meet, high or low,
Man or woman, my parents from long ago.
I treat them all as close brothers and sisters, with love in my heart.
For this the stupid and jealous may mock me,
But they cannot change my naturally kind thoughts.

To the man in the street I am careless and childish, whatever
      happens.
"He is an aimless wanderer. He gives no importance to wealth,"
      they may say.
But distracted by accumulating and protecting this ground of all
      suffering, destruction, and quarrel,
One cuts the vital vein of the virtuous mind,
And one's human life is carried away like paper in the wind:
So I do not cherish much this weapon to kill myself!

Through the kindness of the lama who taught me that there is no
      need for anything,
I do not hope to quench my thirst with the mirage-water of the
      eight worldly concerns.
Since prejudiced praise and blame are like the sound of an echo,
And the human mind like the sun's rays on a snowcapped
      mountain,
Expecting nothing from inferiors, I am not tied to a retinue.
I do not try to catch the colors of the rainbow through not
      understanding its nature,
And even if others do not like me, my mind is happy.

Through the kindness of the lama who introduced me to the
      wisdom bliss of the fulfillment stage,
I took the support of the wisdom consort, the messenger of
      skillful means:
The taste of great bliss, milked from the cow of the sky,
Sealed the aggregates, elements, sense consciousnesses, and all
      things, the universe and beings,
And all appearances arose as the symbol of great bliss.
Happy am I, a yogin enjoying the four joys of great bliss!

Through the kindness of the lama who introduced me to all things
      as illusions,

Appearance was revealed as unobstructed and evanescent in the
endless wheel of illusion,
Sound as the clear and unborn notes of an echo,
And aimless discursive thoughts arising of themselves, and
dispersing and vanishing like clouds.

Kye Ho! Friends! Look at this wonderful show!
In the plain of the absolute nature, from the first, beyond bondage
and freedom,
The son of a barren woman riding the elephant of illusion,
His head adorned with a sky-flower, comes dancing and singing!
Who imposed the pattern of the theories of discursive thought
On phenomenal existence, the manifest dance of the kingly
dharmakaya?
How wonderful is this illusory show of samsara and nirvana!

As the kind teacher who introduced me to the absolute nature as
illusion declared,
"In the primordial wisdom-space, free from dust, pure and
all-pervading,
The realization of the unbiased absolute body is free from falling
into extremes.
What use is meditation that clings to concrete reality and hopes
and fears?"

Even if one remains ordinary, not meditating, who is deluded?
How wonderful is the sky-like yoga of the nonactivity of the
absolute nature!
The childish, clinging to concrete reality, boast about doing things
where there is nothing to do.
They are like thirsty deer trying to reach the water of a mirage.
Poor ignorant creatures, tormented by pointless fatigue!
Through the kindness of the teacher who showed me appearance
and activity as illusion,
When the myriad colored lights of samsara and nirvana,
The self-radiant and unobstructed play of the wisdom of the
absolute space,
Arose in the land of illusion as the play of illusion,
The illusory yogin reached the self-domain of illusion.
What use to him are these illusory dreamlike appearances,

Empty, hollow and without essence, like bamboo,
Insubstantial forms like a moon in water, like visions in the air?

Through the kindness of the teacher who revealed all appearance
    as illusion,
The mist of the discursive judgments of intellectual analysis
And intense attraction to illusory things, dissolved in self-
    liberation,
In the absolute space which is birthless, beyond thought and
    expression.
No more bondage of hope and fear!
No more bondage of adopting and rejection!

Ema! Listen well, dear friends!
Although I am neither shrewd nor clever, this is what I think:
In essence, when the illusory yogin has exhausted acceptance and
    rejection,
Samsara and nirvana arise as an illusory play.
This indeed is the fruit itself, free from all obscurations.
Apart from this, what use is great knowledge and understanding?

Through the kindness of the teacher, the incomparable glorious
    protector, who spoke all this,
I received this legacy of Longchen Rabjam's instructions,
Which is impossible to evaluate in gold and jewels.
Although I think I might, in this mere intellectual way, point
    towards
The realization of the heart-essence of luminous absolute space,
I have not gained the slightest experience of it, not to mention any
    realization.
If I have made mistakes, I confess them to the *yidams* and teachers.

As the lord of the world, Drimé Oser, said,
"Disciples and vajra brothers and sisters long known to me,
Now, when you have the support of the wish-fulfilling jewel
    endowed with freedom and riches,
And the Buddha's doctrine is radiating like a snow mountain in
    its youthful splendor,
All of you, like lion cubs in the prime of youth,
Follow the Buddha, the lion among men!

After bringing experiences and realization to perfection, like the
    snow lion's abundant turquoise mane,
You will soon reach the kingdom of the blissful absolute expanse!"

Even if I, an evil doer, go to hell one day,
I am sure to have the fortune of being freed by the gracious lama,
And I wish and pray that at that time all beings who had a
    connection with me
May enjoy unsurpassable enlightenment
In the beautiful blue lotus buddha-field of the *Tathagata.*
Until then I pray that by the power of relative karma,
We vajra brothers and sisters may meet again and again,
And enjoy the secret teaching of the omniscient teacher,
    Longchenpa,
The ambrosia of the heart-treasure of luminosity.
Moreover, to you the *sangha,* worthy of worship by gods and men,
I offer a white *pundarika* flower, and a prayer:
May your lotus feet remain for oceans of *kalpas,*
And may the myriad light rays of the teaching and practice
    of Dharma
radiate in a hundred directions.

Though self-awareness, the kingly doer of all, is beyond
    movement and effort,
These words, sincere bearers of my news, are its self-manifesta-
    tion, the dancing song of the mind's child:
They came from the palace of the deep red tent within the breast,[1]
In the great mountain citadel of the body,
Through the secret way of the sixteen-petalled enjoyment *chakra,*[2]
Sent on a path of white paper as dazzling as a snowy mountain,
To the monastery of Namling Shedrub in the Sandalwood Forest.[3]

Nyoshul Khen Rinpoche. Dechen Choling, East Meredith,
New York, 1992. Photo: Kedar Harris.

Nyoshul Khen Rinpoche in Tibet with his nephew, his wife, Damchö Zangmo, and Surya Das. Photo courtesy of the author.

Nyoshul Khen Rinpoche and Surya Das. Santa Fe, 1993. Photo: Kedar Harris.

The late Nyingma leaders and Dzogchen masters, H.H. Dudjom Rinpoche and H.H. Dilgo Khyentse Rinpoche. Dordogne, France, 1984. Photo: Ven. Matthieu Ricard.

H.H. Dilgo Khyentse Rinpoche, Nyoshul Khenpo (in center), and H.E. Shechen Rabjam Rinpoche. Paris, France, early 1980s. Photo: Ven. Matthieu Ricard.

11   A Spontaneous Song To My Wife: Sacred Heart Essence of Pith-Instructions

Advice in the Form of a Song,
to My Wife Damchö Zangmo

Translated by Surya Das, David Christensen,
and Corinna Chung, 1986

Homage to the guru.

To the embodiment of the king of Dharma, Longchen Rabjam,
To the lord of buddha-families, Shedrub Tenpai Nyima,[4]
To the two incomparable great *tertons*,[5] other lamas, and my twenty-
    five supreme spiritual guides,
I respectfully bow.

This advice is to my heart-friend Damchö Zangmo and others, and
the disciples who rely upon me.

I

In this life we have obtained a splendid, free, and well-endowed
    human body,
Met with a supreme, authentic teacher,
And received the ambrosial instructions of the aural transmission.
At this time, without leaving our three doors[6] in indifference,
Practice to achieve perfect enlightenment in the following way:

First, with the five perceptions[7] of the teacher as the Buddha and
    so forth,
Upon the crown of one's head or in one's heart,
Visualize the incomparable, kind lord of Dharma, the lama,
With devotion intense enough to make your hairs quiver,
Praying with a melodious, yearning call,
And then take the four empowerments, mingling your mind
    with his.

All the numberless *sadhanas* of the Victorious Buddhas without
    exception,
If condensed, are the *guru yoga*, it is said.
In all the great secret, definitive sutras and tantras,
And especially the Dzogchen tantras,
This "Method of the All-Embodying Jewel" is superlatively praised.
Therefore, we should rely, as if on one's own heart, on a loving
    teacher,
Who is composed, disciplined, and perfectly peaceful,
Endowed with superior virtuous qualities and enriched by
    scriptural knowledge.

If we don't rely upon this precious embodiment of all refuges,
It will be impossible to attain enlightenment.
How can a blind man travel without a guide?
Therefore, continuously pray to the great guide to liberation,
My heart-friends.

Refuge is the foundation of the Dharma,
Without it, it is impossible to enter the mansion of liberation.
Considering the teacher as our companion on the way,
By possessing the three faiths,[8] one should always cry for refuge.
Heart-friends, don't mistake the basis of the sacred Dharma!

If we lack mindfulness, we will be destroyed
By thieving demons.
All the countless positive actions in this and future lives
Are accomplished through mindfulness,
So always remember alert presence of mind,
My heart-friends!

The way out of this cyclic existence,
The great entrance to the path of liberation,
And the initial step for all Dharma practices,
Is genuine renunciation alone, it is said.
So reflect deeply on renunciation,
My heart-friends!

During childhood, distracted by play;
In the prime of life, youthful body distracted by desire;
White-haired and full of wrinkles, close to death:
This human life passes futilely, my heart-friends!

In this world, each minute of time,
Day and night, each instant is fleeting.
Some are being born, some are dying,
Some are happy, and some are miserable,
Some are crying, some laugh, and so on:
Seeing all things are as impermanent as a flash of lightning,
It's so sad to stay lax and unconcerned,
Assuming that you have obtained the power of adamantine life
And will live until Lord Maitreya's coming—
So don't remain indifferent, my heart-friends!

The nature of everything is illusory and ephemeral.
Those with dualistic perception regard suffering as happiness,
Like those who lick honey from the edge of a razor blade.
How pitiful, those who cling strongly to concrete reality!
Turn your attention within, my heart-friends!

When you are happy, everything seems very pleasant,
When you're not, all is threatening and oppressive,
Human moods are like the highlights and shadows on a sunlit
    mountain range.
There is no one to depend upon in this time,
So point your finger to yourself, my heart-friends!

This free and well-endowed human life is like a wish-granting
    jewel,
Don't return empty-handed from this island of jewels,
My heart-friends!

Here in this great city of the six realms of being,
Comparable to an island of demonesses or a nest of vipers,
Or an excruciating fire pit,
Consider how suffering continually oppresses, my heart-friends!

Both the vital life-force and one's life-span are rushing by like the
    water of a steep mountain cascade,
Impermanence swiftly approaches, my heart-friends.
The three realms of samsara are like an inescapable prison,
So don't be overly attached to cyclic existence,
My heart-friends!

Relying on fickle friends is like chasing after rainbows:
When you need them, they are no help, my heart-friends.
All compounded phenomena are like lightning flashes in the sky,
So don't rely on anything, my heart-friends.
One's family is transient, like visitors at a marketplace,
So don't squabble and bear ill will towards them, my heart-friends!

Possessions are ephemeral, like dew on the grass,
So give generously to spiritual causes, my heart-friends.
The only beneficial thing is the sublime, divine Dharma,
So don't fool yourselves, my heart-friends.
The perpetual refuge is an authentic teacher,
So don't be hypocritical regarding your *samaya*, my heart-friends!

If you cut off the head, the body can accomplish nothing,
If you damage your samaya, you will not accomplish the purpose
    of the Dharma.
Therefore, by constantly maintaining alertness, awareness, and
    vigilance,
Protect your samaya, my heart-friends.
If one is pure within, all will be pure without,
So have pure vision regarding all things, my heart-friends!

The supreme field of merit, and exemplars of the way, is the
    guiding sangha,
So don't fall into wrong views and criticism, my heart-friends.
However imperfect a disciple of the Buddha may become,
One hundred ordinary beings will still not match him,
So always serve and respect them, my heart-friends!

Since you do not know which beings are spiritually exalted,
Don't grab in the dark like a blind man, my heart-friends.
As you don't know where the hidden *yogis* abide,
You ought to revere all, my heart-friends!

From a small positive action, a great benefit will arise,
So don't scorn actions that are simple, my heart-friends.
Whoever, merely hearing the name of the Buddha,
Just raises one hand in respect,
Will have planted the seed of perfect enlightenment, it is said,
So never be mistaken, my heart-friends!

If we fail to acknowledge the teacher in his presence,
And then pray to him from afar, it is too late.
When we have a lama but don't meditate on his pith-instructions,
There's no point in having futile thoughts afterwards, my
     heart-friends.
If you don't accomplish the divine Dharma in this life,
In future lives it will be difficult, my heart-friends!

O, all the ignorant beings of the three realms wander
In transmigration, between the fangs of the impermanence-
     demoness of three-fold existence,
But alas!—they don't realize this.
Tomorrow or this evening, who knows when death will come?
Still, no one worries about it,
But remains careless and complacent.
Oh, how pitiful the way beings deceive themselves!

Tomorrow or your next existence,
Who knows which will come first?
If you don't keep the lama's pith-instructions in mind,
You will only deceive yourselves, my heart-friends!

Turn your attention within, scrutinize yourself,
And undertake what is meaningful, you who are called my
     heart-friends.
Quickly, quickly, practice the transcendent Dharma, and don't look
     to the future,
Immediately practice the sublime Dharma, my heart-friends!

II

The door of the Dharma is renunciation,
so karmically connected Damchö Zangmo,
Listen once again, my heart-friend.

The lordly Buddha Longchen Rabjam said,
"All the teachings of the Buddhas are condensed
In the pith-instructions on the practical application of the three
    excellences"—
The preparatory, main, and concluding practices,
Which are the veritable life-force of the path.
So the way to practice these is as follows:

If they are present, it's sufficient for the accomplishment of
    buddhahood,
If they're absent, there will be no way to accomplish
    enlightenment.
They are the infallible seed for accomplishing buddhahood.

The pure and supremely precious bodhicitta,
Which is uncontrived, should arise in your being,
Without this, there is no way to attain buddhahood.
So, firstly, the excellent preparation of generating the altruistic mind
    of enlightenment is important.

Of all beings in the universe,
None have not been your parents.
Through their great kindness they formed our body,
Gave life and material goods,
And showed us the ways of the world.

Although they desire only happiness,
They are like a blind person without a guiding friend.
In order that all beings, tormented in unbearable cyclic existence,
Accomplish everlasting peace, unsurpassable enlightenment,
Motivated by the altruistic objective of the twofold benefit with
    both its aspects,[9]
You should generate the supreme mind, intent upon attaining
    perfect enlightenment.

This bodhicitta is the all-sufficient wish-fulfilling jewel,
This is the foundation of all the vast and profound teachings,
This is the central point of all the paths of sutra and tantra.

One aspect of the nature of the two truths
Is the relative level, the principal theme of all practice,
The king of all supreme methods.
Without this, there is no other means to accomplish buddhahood.
If you lack either method or wisdom,
How will the path be accomplished?

Of the two supreme paths, first
The path of skillful means is praised.
For the preparation on the path, generate the bodhicitta:
"This has immeasurable benefits," the all-knowing Lord Maitreya
    said to Norzang.

The bodhicitta is like the moon which eliminates darkness.
Bodhicitta is like the all-illumining sun.
Bodhicitta protects from the terrors of samsara.
Bodhicitta repels the obstacles of the four demons.[10]
Bodhicitta eliminates the fever of the five poisons.[11]
Bodhicitta acts as the stallion of endeavor.
Bodhicitta is the sturdy armor of patience.

Bodhicitta discards all moral downfalls.
Bodhicitta supports the accomplishment of meditative
    concentration.
Bodhicitta gives birth to excellent tranquillity.
Bodhicitta causes supreme wisdom to arise in the mind.

Bodhicitta perfects the great accumulations of merit.
Bodhicitta brings forth the view of emptiness.
When bodhicitta is present, the moon of skillful means rises.
If you meditate on bodhicitta, the sun of penetrating insight is
    evident.

If you meditate on bodhicitta, pristine awareness fully unfolds.
By bodhicitta, the benefit of others effortlessly arises.
Through bodhicitta, the qualities of the ten bodhisattva levels are
    perfected.

All the relative qualities and the one hundred and twelve freedoms
Of the great bodhisattvas dwelling on the first level,
Up to the innumerable, ineffable, immeasurable
Wisdom-eyes, clairvoyances, miraculous powers and so forth,
As well as the thirty-two major and eighty minor signs
Of the countless *Sugatas'* golden bodies and so on—
All these enlightened qualities arising from the accumulation
    of merit,
Stem from the power of supreme, unsurpassable bodhicitta.

Bodhicitta subdues the demon of ego-clinging.
Bodhicitta frees from the prison of samsara.
Bodhicitta evaporates the ocean of suffering.
Bodhicitta equalizes suffering and happiness.

Bodhicitta is like a brave escort.
Bodhicitta is like the great fire at the end of an eon.
Bodhicitta is like the best fruit of a marvelous tree.
Bodhicitta opens the door to the treasury of altruism.

Lacking such profound and supreme bodhicitta,
Like powerful Ram, who dwelt twelve years in the forest,
But was driven by the goad of attachment to fight his enemies,
Or like Gelong Thangpa, who, although he could fly freely in
    the sky
By having mastered energy and mind, started a battle,
The fault was the absence of unsurpassable bodhicitta.

Brahma himself, even after attaining desireless bliss,
Will become blazing firewood in Avici hell,
And Indra, although venerated by the entire world,
By the power of karma will fall back to the ground.
Lacking the kingly mountain of bodhicitta is the fault.

In this world, so many of those glorified by the highest rank,
Like great kings, generals, prime ministers, and presidents,
Finally destroyed themselves and others.
The fault lay with the rotten root of bodhicitta.

Innumerable *shravakas, pratyekabuddhas,* and hosts of other
    superior beings
Possessed the two hundred fifty vows of pure ethical discipline.
But although beautified by the three trainings,[12] related practices,
    experience, and realization,
Without bodhicitta, the root of all Dharma,
Sometimes, liberating only themselves, they remained in great
    peace.

From among all the vast divisions of the Buddha's teachings,
Bodhicitta is the very quintessence.
Bodhicitta repels the harm of the lower realms.
Bodhicitta reveals the supreme path of liberation.

"If the yogin possesses bodhicitta,
Even if he doesn't accomplish any virtue through body and speech,
He will not stray from the path of liberation."
Thus said Chokyi Wangpo,[13] who has mastered the five sciences.

"The five heinous evils and so on, all great negative actions,
Will be overpowered by the unsurpassable bodhicitta,
And all the lesser sins will also be removed,"
Said the great Indian pandit Shantideva.

"Whoever abides in the supreme bodhicitta,
Their life will be regarded as a pleasant garden,
Whether successful or even destitute,
The miseries of the lower realms won't terrify,"
Lord Maitreya stated in the *Sutra-alamkara.*

In brief, the unsurpassable precious bodhicitta
Is the heart-essence of all the Buddhas of the three times.
Since without it there is no way to accomplish enlightenment,
It is the authentic root of the path
Of sutras, tantras, and pith-instructions.

This excellent preparatory practice of generating bodhicitta
Is praised with one voice by all the millions of past holy ones.
It should not become mere intellectual knowledge,

But should be reflected upon again and again,
And united with your being, my heart-friends!

Don't be distracted, don't be distracted—train in bodhicitta.
Don't be mistaken, don't be mistaken—train in bodhicitta.
Don't err, don't err—train in bodhicitta.

If the foundation of bodhicitta is not firm,
The extremely profound essential pith-instructions of the creative
   and completion phases,
And other practices, will be difficult to perfect.
Therefore the preparatory generation of bodhicitta is the starting
   point on the Path.

III

Listen again, my heart-friends!

Second is the *excellence* of the nonconceptualized main practice,
The profound views of Mahamudra, Mahasandhi, and
   Madhyamika.
Without this, all practices are essenceless, like a mere reflection,
Like blind people without a guide, it is said.

The complementary aspect of means is wisdom; this sublime path
Is the practice of emptiness, the absolute truth.
Whoever does not strive to practice this,
How can he fly with only one wing of the pair of means and
   wisdom?
Therefore, the excellent non-conceptualized main practice is
   important.

All concepts about the ground are cut by Madhyamika;
The pith-instruction of the path is Mahamudra;
The ultimate result is the Great Perfection.
My karmically connected Lady Damchö Zangmo,
Here is the way to meditate on these practices:

Not like a butterfly fluttering in the sky,
But through the pith-instructions, Like the Great Garuda Soaring
   In Space,
Powerfully cut all limitations with the sovereign view.

Not just with the efforts of insistent fools,
But through the pith-instructions, The Cycle of the *Dharmata* of the
Three Essential Points,
Stabilize the sovereign meditation, one's intrinsic nature.

Not just through futile, foolish action,
But through the pith-instructions of Arriving at the Great Equal
Taste,
Equalize the flavors of samsara and nirvana with sovereign
action.

Not like the light of a firefly,
But through the pith-instructions of The Uneclipsed and
Unobscured Sun and Moon,
Recognize clearly intrinsic awareness, the sovereign result.

Listen again, my heart-friends!

The heart-essence of the Victorious Buddhas of the three times,
The most secret of the *Great Secret Dakinis' Treasure*,
The most refined light of the Seventeen Tantras of Luminosity,
The essential quintessence of the *One Hundred Nineteen Pith-
Instructions*,
The most vital condensed point among all the vital points,
Is the perfect Buddha Drimé Oser's[14] *Treasury of Aural Lineage
Pith-Instructions*:

The Pith-Instruction of Cracking the Shell of Ignorance.
The Pith-Instruction of Cutting the Net of Confusion.
The Pith-Instruction of Sky-like Equality.
The Pith-Instruction Which Demolishes the Hut of Duality.
The Pith-Instruction Which Shows the Distinction Between Samsara
and Nirvana.
The Pith-Instruction Which Instantaneously Shows Intrinsic
Awareness.
The Pith-Instruction Which Essentializes One Hundred Vital Points.
The Pith-Instruction Which Clarifies the Way to Maintain
Meditative Experiences.
The Pith-Instruction Which Reveals the Single Knowledge
Which Liberates All.

The Cycle of the Brahmin Which Discriminates With Kingly
    Certainty.
And the Pith-Instruction Which Actually Reveals Spontaneous-
    Liberation, and so on.

These should not be just merely theoretical.
Rather, pierce the heart of the continuing delusion of ignorance
With the essential meaning of the three incisive words.

Listen again, my heart-friends!

Don't contrive, don't contrive, don't alter your mind,
Adopting manipulation and modification,
Mind will be disturbed,
And this contrived state of mind
Will obscure the heart of the matter.

Mind-itself, free of fabrication, is one's authentic, original
    countenance.
Gaze nakedly at this intrinsic nature, without alteration,
Preserving the flow of meditation,
Free of adulteration by artifice.

All phenomena are contained in the infinity of samsara and
    nirvana,
One is perfect, two are perfect,
All are perfect in the mind:
Remain in the innate nature of mind, Great Perfection.
One is liberated, two are liberated,
All are liberated in their own place:
Remain in the naturally liberated state, Great Perfection.

Free of distraction, free of clinging, free of meditation, beyond
    intellect:
Remain in the state beyond intellect, Great Perfection.
Selfless, unborn, free of extremes, inexpressible:
Remain in the ineffable nature, Great Perfection.

Primordially present, naturally occurring, all is spontaneously
    perfect:
Remain in the spontaneous equality of the Great Perfection.

Equally true, equally pure, all are equal:
Remain in the equality of the Great Perfection.

All pervading, spacious dharmata, the great sky:
Remain in the state of Great Perfection, vast as space.
Free from the cage of change, agent of change, and anything to
    change,
Remain in the state of uncontrived great spontaneity.

Remaining uncontrived, you will meet the self-arisen deity.
Remaining in nonmeditation, you will accomplish naturally
    inherent buddhahood.
In the nonexisting expanse of intrinsic awareness wisdom,
Remain in the state of self-arisen Kuntuzangpo.[15]

The absolute bodhicitta is pure like the sky,
The sun of intrinsic awareness wisdom is primordially apparent,
The primordially present self-arisen Kuntuzangpo.
You may think it's eternal, but it's not,
You may see it as nonexistent, but it's not,
And the same regarding both and neither, and so on.
The undifferentiated, unified, sky-like nature of mind.
Childish mentalities doubt whether they are mistaken or not.

Pure from the beginning, concerning the meaning of the great
    dharmakaya—
Analyzing it by intellectual processes,
Even if we search
Till the end of the eon, we won't find it.
Uninformed, childish folk, trying to tie knots in the sky:
O, how pitiable, these ignorant ones!
In brief, what's the point of making many elaborations?

Wherever there is a reference point, there's a poisonous view,
Wherever there is fixation, there's said to be a treacherous path of
    meditation,
If there is adopting and rejecting, there is faulty action,
Where there is a goal in mind, the result will be hindered:
Simply remain in a state of nondistraction, free of clinging and
    grasping.

Whatever the object of meditation, whoever meditates,
Whatever the method, however we meditate, and so on....
Go beyond all these in the *dharmadhatu,*
The primordially present expanse of wisdom-mind,
Samantabhadra's nonaction.

Whoever is without clinging
To the dualistic extremes of meditating
And not meditating,
Reaches the great nondual state beyond intellect.

The dharmata cannot even partially be shown by writing,
And even by lengthy explanations it is difficult to perceive:
Homogenous purity, primordial sameness,
Great equal taste,
Nonacting primordially occurring space of Kuntuzangpo.

Rest at ease in the infinite vast expanse,
And don't rely on the hardships of hundreds of paths.
Then the sun of Drimé Oser Kuntuzangpo's wisdom-mind
Will certainly dawn in your heart,
So, essentialize hundreds of crucial points into one, my
    heart-friends!

The dharmakaya is ever-unchanging.
Like the blind bird searching for the limits of the sky,
Or a blind person examining an elephant's body,
One will never find the limits of the unelaborated dharmata.

The absolute being effortless, don't strive too much,
Give up the nine actions[16] of contrived practices,
And remain in the vast, natural primordial flow.
Without relying on the various contrived paths,
One accomplishes Buddhahood in one lifetime,
The ultimate, uncontrived, absolute fruit.
Thus it's been said by Drimé Oser and others,
As well as one hundred thousand accomplished *vidyadharas,*
So keep the import of this in mind, my heart-friends!

Hey, if your eyes are open, don't jump off the cliff!
Don't abandon the sovereign, and expect something elsewhere!

Don't leave the elephant, and search for its footprints!
Don't throw away the kernel and keep the husk!

Similar to the special qualities that distinguish gold from brass,
The truth of the difference between mind and rigpa will be
    obvious when you apply the practice.
Intrinsic awareness, the sovereign wish-granting jewel,
Is the quintessential advice of the heart, my heart-friends.

IV

The concluding practice is the *excellence* of dedicating the merits.

Taking whatever merit is accomplished here as an example,
and gathering it together with all the merit accumulated through
    out the three times
By ourselves and all sentient beings—
Both that which is referential and that which is endowed with the
    nonreferential three-fold purity[17]—
Just as the hosts of Buddhas and bodhisattvas perfectly dedicate
    their merits
For all beings without exception, limitless like the sky,
To swiftly obtain unsurpassable, perfect enlightenment,
Seal this merit with an excellent prayer of pure dedication.

By this, the roots of merit will not be destroyed by circumstances,
But increase many times over until enlightenment.

This unique mark of distinction, not found with other teachers,[18]
Is praised extensively in the sutras, tantras, and *shastras*,
Such as the *Avatamsaka Sutra*, the *One Hundred Thousand Verse
    Prajnaparamita*,
The *Sutra of the Cycle of Perfect Dedication*, and so on.
All the infinite teachings of the Buddhas, without exception,
Are condensed in this practice of the three *excellences*:
The excellent generation of bodhicitta as preparation,
The excellent nonconceptual meditative practice,
and dedicating the merits as conclusion.

The lordly Buddha Longchen Rabjam's

Pith-Instructions of the Extraordinary Path states,
"The preparatory generation of the enlightened mind,
The unconceptualized main practice,
And concluding with the dedication, all thoroughly applied:
These are three invaluables for traversing the path of liberation."
Thus says *The Treasury of the Wish-Fulfilling Jewel.*

At the time of the ground, these are the nature of the two truths,
During the path, the perfection of the two accumulations, merit
    and wisdom,
At the time of the fruit, the accomplishment of dharmakaya and
    rupakaya, and so on,
They are the heart-essence of all the Buddha's teachings.

More than this is unnecessary, less is insufficient.
These three invaluables are the heart and life of the path,
thus, place them in your heart, beloved one.

This pith-instruction, superior to the elixir of the heart,
Was composed through heartfelt love as sincere advice
To the spouse and companion of my heart, Damcho Zangmo.
May it auspiciously transform into the heart's ambrosia!

This was sung in Dordogne, the land of great bliss,
In the forest of self-arising Kuntuzangpo,
In the hut of totally spacious blue sky,
And offered by the dog among men, a human form among dogs,
The bad monk, ragged Jamyang Dorje:

By these merits, your heart flowing into the meaning of dharmata,
May this be the cause of actualizing the dharmakaya wisdom mind.
Moreover, from now until enlightenment—
Unlike the virtueless, ignorant, worldly people
Who behave like dogs and pigs, fighting and quarreling in
    benighted cities,
Persistently struggling on and on, burdened by suffering—
Through integrating all pleasures into the path of the secret
    Mantrayana teaching,
Mind at ease within the swift protection of the secret path,

May we enjoy vajra dances and songs,
Perfect skill in experiencing the wisdom of the emptiness-bliss of
    the four joys,
Actualize the great bliss of awareness-itself,
And may our body, possessions, and all the assembled merits of
    the three times,
Sustain the practice which accomplishes enlightenment.

May this wish, not mere words,
But my heartfelt prayer,
Be granted by the hosts of Buddhas and bodhisattvas!

So, for now, from the great western kingdom of France,
This advice is to my beloved wife Damchö Zangmo and others:
May it be virtuous!

12   The Essential Meaning
Dordogne, France 1983

I bow to the *Bhagavan* king of the sky!

Kye Ho! Listen, my best heart-friend,
Intelligent and learned excellent sun:

Give up all distractions, all the many spreading delusions,
And for an instant look at absolute reality, as it is.
Today, in front, behind, and so on,
In the ten directions, above and below,
All three varieties of perceptions—outer, inner, and intermediate—
However they appear, all these are absolute reality as it is, and its
    natural expression,
None other than creative display.

Inwardly, watch the nature of your mind,
Sky-like effortless natural mind,
Nature as-it-is, spontaneously pure from the very beginning,
Absolute truth, beyond accomplishment through effort with cause
    and conditions,
Great gnosis of self-luminosity, innate wakefulness, one's own
    intrinsic awareness,
Transcending all the inhibitions, dwelling upon, coming and
    going,
The natural state free from concepts, mental projections, and
    absorptions.

Everything is the natural flow, great spontaneous immanence,
Gnosis beyond thought, expression, and example,
Buddha's mind, nature of the great vast expanse,
Wisdom-mind of self-born Kuntuzangpo,
The ultimate reach of all the dharmas,
Sutras, tantras, transmissions, and pith-instructions,
Praised by the millions of past learned and accomplished ones,
Not only once but again and again.
This I request you to make the heart of all practices.

Regarding the correct meditation on this meaning:
The starting point of the practice is faith and the desire to be free
    from samsara.
The ground of the practice is the four mind changes.[19]
The foundation of the practice is refuge and bodhicitta.
The guardian of the practice is the perfectly pure dedication prayer.
These are the profound vital points of all the paths of the sutras
    and tantras.
As they make us reach the ultimate point of the path of practice,
They are its root and should not be lost.
Therefore, my heart-son, I request you to keep it in your
    heart-mind!

If one goes to the essence, all this will be included,
If not, then all the knowledge and studies,
Even though one perseveres in them for *kalpas,* will only be a cause
    of weariness.

This brief essential instruction is spoken
By me, the evil lawless man Jamyang Dorje.
I offer this advice which is like my heart
To you, my best, beloved heart-friend.
Do not relinquish it, but treasure it in your heart.
By this merit, may your mind enjoy practicing
Continuously, without separation, the essential meaning!
This is advice to the American Dharma practitioner called Surya,
who is learned in Buddhist and non-Buddhist scriptural traditions.

   Géo!
   Mangalam!

History

Gyalwa Longchenpa with Samantabhadra and Samantabhadri in heart-center.
Painted by Madeleine Carré, with Nyoshul Khenpo's guidance, for the Long-
chenpa Sadhana, "Tiglé Gyachen." Photo: Madeleine Carré.

13   The Dzogchen Lineage of Nyoshul Khenpo

by Surya Das

The teachings and practice of Ati Dzogpa Chenpo, the Great Perfection, descend from two peerless eighth century Indian tantric masters, Guru Rinpoche and Vimalamitra, down through a distinguished lineage of learned and accomplished Tibetan masters, as well as through visionary revelations. In the fourteenth century, the teachings merge in the omniscient Longchen Rabjam, also known as Gyalwa Longchenpa, the pre-eminent mind of the Ancient School, the Nyingmapas. This Dzogchen tradition is known as the Earlier Dzogchen Nyingthig or Heart-Essence.

Rigdzin Jigme Lingpa was the spiritual heir of Longchen Rabjam. In the eighteenth century he received the complete teachings and transmissions of the Dzogchen Nyingthig in visions from Manjushrimitra (Jampel Shenyen), Guru Rinpoche, Vimalamitra, and Gyalwa Longchenpa. In three clear visions of Longchenpa, Jigme Lingpa received the blessings of his incomparable guru, inseparable from the primordial Buddha Samantabhadra (Kuntuzangpo in Tibetan), and attained enlightenment.

Gyalwa Longchenpa composed over two hundred works, some of which are still extant. Rigdzin Jigme Lingpa's illumined writings, such as *Yonten Rinpoche Dzeu*, contain the condensed essence of all of Gyalwa Longchenpa's inexhaustible instructions and commentaries, including Longchenpa's renowned *Seven Treasures*. In essence, these writings include all the innumerable Buddha-dharmas. The *termas*, rediscovered Dharma treasures—which Jigme Lingpa received on five (or seven) yellow scrolls, as well as mystically, mind to mind—form the basis for the tradition known as Longchen Nyingthig, the Heart Essence of the Vast Expanse. This is also known as the Later Dzogchen Nyingthig tradition.

Details concerning Gyalwa Longchenpa, Rigdzin Jigme Lingpa, and the other forefathers of the Dzogchen lineage stemming from Samantabhadra and Garab Dorje, are described in many other books and teachings. This chapter briefly describes the Longchen Nyingthig lineage as received and taught by Nyoshul Khenpo Jamyang Dorje, descending from Rigdzin Jigme Lingpa in a continuous stream of blessings. This is the heart-essence of omniscient Longchenpa and Rigdzin Jigme Lingpa, the extremely short and direct particular lineage of Longchen Nyingthig, the terma of Jigme Lingpa, the fresh breath of the *dakinis*, Dorje Sempa's vajra-shortcut.

First, a brief description of the general Dzogchen lineage, the long lineage or *ringyu*. This lineage descends from the primordial Buddha Kuntuzangpo, to Dorje Sempa, Garab Dorje, Jampel Shenyen, Shri Simha, Jñanasutra, Vimalamitra, and Padmasambhava, and includes numerous enlightened lamas who followed in their footsteps. All this is chronicled in the long lineage of *kahma*, explained below. For the names of these root lineage lamas, see the lineage prayer by Nyoshul Khenpo, entitled *Osel sangwa nyingthig gi gyupai soldeb mutig trengwa, The Luminous Secret Heart-Essence Pearl Rosary Lineage Prayer*.

According to the general lineage of Dzogchen Nyingthig, between the eighth century Indian *pandita* Vimalamitra and Longchenpa, there were one dozen exalted root lineage holders, and between Longchenpa and Jigme Lingpa there were fourteen. This considers only the main lineage holders, not the other accomplished ones who accompanied them. This long lineage of Dzogpa Chenpo thus descends from the primordial Buddha Kuntuzangpo, from teacher to student, in an unbroken stream through today.

HOW THE TEACHINGS WERE TRANSMITTED

The teachings of the Nyingma or Old Translation School are transmitted through two main systems, the kahma and the terma lineages. *Kahma* refers to all the teachings and transmissions passed down through the centuries by the long lineage of teachers and disciples. *Terma* refers to the previously hidden, rediscovered teachings of the short and direct lineage (*nyegyu*) from Guru Rinpoche and other enlightened ones. These masters transmit teachings directly, through their deathless wisdom-bodies, in visionary experience, to the *terton* who discovers and reveals these teachings. Such a short, fresh, direct, extremely powerful, and profound transmission is the terma of Jigme Lingpa's *Longchen Nyingthig*. Of the nine volumes of Jigme Lingpa's writings, two are *gong ter*, wisdom-mind treasures.

Jigme Lingpa said that there are four purposes for the discovery of terma: so the Dharma won't disappear; so that the essential instructions don't become adulterated over long periods of time, when mistakes and breaches of commitments and misunderstanding might take place; so that the blessings do not fade; and, so that the direct lineage of transmission is maintained. The terma provide teachings by Guru Rinpoche Padmasambhava that are appropriate to the various needs and natures of different people in different places and times.

One can obtain the ultimate fruit of the path by practicing one particular terma alone, for each is complete in itself. Yet in order to preserve and uphold all the teachings of the Buddhadharma in their totality, one must also receive the kahma lineage transmission. Therefore, the kahma and terma are generally practiced and passed on inseparably.

Dzogchen teachings are generally classified into three main categories: *Sem De*, Mind Class; *Long De*, Expanse Class; and *Men Ngag Gi De*, Pith-Instructions Class. This threefold classification was made by Jampel Shenyen, Garab Dorje's disciple.

Twenty-one major tantras form the basis of Sem De. Nine tantras (divided into groups of three: white, black, and multicolored) form the basis of Long De. The Men Ngag Gi De category is subdivided into four subsections. The fourth of these, *Gyu Rangshung*, is the text of root tantras and explanatory tantras in the most complete, essentialized form. These are the pith-instructions proper.

The subsection of Gyu Rangshung in Men Ngag Gi De is itself divided into four groups known as *Thigle Korshi*. These four are *Chikor*, Outer Cycle; *Nangkor*, Inner Cycle; *Sangkor*, Secret Cycle; and *Yangsang Lame*, Supersecret and Highest. This fourfold classification was made by Shri Simha, Jampel Shenyen's disciple.

Nyingthig is short for *Nying Gi Thigle*, meaning Heart-Essence or Innermost Essence. It refers to the most quintessential pith-instructions (*men ngag*) of Ati Dzogpa Chenpo. The term "nyingthig" pertains solely to the Men Ngag Gi De, the pith-instructions group of Dzogchen teachings. Moreover, it often refers in particular to the innermost or most profound and secret core of those pith-instructions, known as Yangsang Lame. Therefore, these teachings are also known as *Sangwa Nyingthig* (Secret Heart-Essence), *Osel Nyingthig* (Luminous Innermost Essence), or *Men Ngag Nyingthig* (Heart-Essence of the Pith-Instructions). Each of these terms refers to the unique Nyingthig teachings found primarily in the Yangsang Lame section of the Men Ngag Gi De.

The seventeen main tantras of Men Ngag Gi De form the basis for the Yangsang Lame. (According to the tradition of Vimalamitra, there are eighteen tantras; according to Guru Rinpoche's tradition, there are nineteen. These are mostly the same tantras, with very slight variations; both masters received this transmission from Shri Simha.) These tantras are found in the thirty-six volume collection of Nyingma tantras, called the *Nyingma Gyubum*, that were compiled by Terchen Ratna Lingpa, the greatest of the thirteen supreme *lingpas*, tertons or treasure masters.

It is difficult for ordinary beings to understand the tantras without the explanations of a qualified teacher. Gyalwa Longchenpa's *Seven Treasures* (*Dzodun*) was written in order to elucidate the extraordinarily profound meaning of the seventeen main tantras of Dzogpa Chenpo, as well as the teachings of all nine vehicles (*yana*). For the purpose of the actual practice of Dzogchen according to these tantras, Longchenpa gathered his own termas, as well as those of Chetsun Senge Wangchuk (who was later reborn as Jamyang Khyentse Wangpo), and Pema Ladrey Tsel (Longchenpa's previous incarnation), in the form of the thirteen volume collection known as the *Nyingthig Yabshi*. This *Yabshi* is the practice aspect of

Longchenpa's writings and the basis of the Old Nyingthig. In it he synthesized the *Bima Nyingthig* of Vimalamitra and the *Khandro Nyingthig* of Guru Rinpoche, and explained all the practical details in the light of his own realization.

The condensed essence of all the tantric teachings elucidated in the *Seven Treasures* of Longchenpa is contained in Jigme Lingpa's poetic *Yonten Dzo, The Treasury of Enlightened Qualities*. The practices included in the *Nyingthig Yabshi* are condensed in a form that is easy to apply, in Jigme Lingpa's four volume *Nyingthig Tsapod*, which includes the renowned *Triyig Yeshe Lama*. This core teaching of the Tsapod is the basis of the extraordinary Dzogchen Togal practice of the Longchen Nyingthig.

These rare and extraordinarily profound teachings precisely explain various essential methods for directly actualizing the innermost teachings of Ati Dzogpa Chenpo, the Great Perfection, the Peak Vehicle, which is the direct method for swiftly realizing the ultimate nature of the mind, and attaining Buddhahood in the rainbow-light body. In modern times, the Longchen Nyingthig is the main practice at the center of all these Dzogchen teachings and pith-instructions.

RIGDZIN JIGME LINGPA

Known as an omniscient *vidyadhara* or "awareness holder," Rigdzin Jigme Lingpa (1729-1798) spent two years doing mantra recitations and prayers, and then received Dzogchen teachings from Lama Thugchog Tsel on the profound text of *Drolthig Gongpa Rangdrol, The Liberating Essence of Innately Free Wisdom Mind*. Then Jigme Lingpa went to a cave near Samye Chimpu for many years, where he prayed constantly to Gyalwa Longchenpa.

During his second three-year retreat, Jigme Lingpa experienced three radiant visions of Longchenpa. In the first he was blessed by Longchenpa's wisdom body, in the second by his wisdom speech, and in the third by his wisdom mind. His mind and Longchenpa's mixed inseparably, and in one instant he understood all of the sutras and tantras completely and infallibly. The details of this story are found in entire volumes written about him. There is a whole volume written about him. His practice and teachings remain our principle inspiration in the Nyingthig tradition today. (His biography is dealt with by Steven Goodman in his article, "Rig-'dzin 'Jigs-med gling-pa and the *kLong Chen sNying-Thig*," in *Tibetan Budhism: Reason and Revelation*, edited by Steven D. Goodman and Ronald M. Davidson.)

In order to swiftly attain realization, one needs the blessing of the guru. This is called *chinlab kyi gyud*, the lineage of blessings. Jigme Lingpa's mystical mind-transmission from the Buddha Longchenpa, who had lived three centuries before, is an example of such waves of inspiration. After these experiences, Jigme Lingpa's writings were on a par with Longchenpa's, although Jigme Lingpa himself had hardly studied texts and commentaries.

We can also look to the story of Rabjam Orgyen Chodrak, who was the guru of Jigme Lingpa's Nyingthig guru, Shri Natha (Rabjam Orgyen Palgon or Lama Palgon). Unfortunately there is no extant spiritual biography (*namthar*) of either of these two lineage masters.

DISCIPLES OF RIGDZIN JIGME LINGPA

Rigdzin Jigme Lingpa had four main enlightened disciples, as prophesied: the so-called "four Jigmes" or "fearless ones." They were Jigme Gyalwai Nyugu, Jigme Thrinley Odzer (the first Dodrup Chen), Jigme Ngotsel Tenzin, and Jigme Kundrol Namgyal. The lineages of the latter pair did not flourish widely; they are now indistinguishable from the two main streams of Longchen Nyingthig, as represented today by the direct lineal descendants of Gyalwai Nyugu and the first Dodrup Chen.

Gyalwai Nyugu's renowned disciple, Dza Patrul Rinpoche (1808-1887) had four main disciples, each of whom became *chodak* or dharma heir of one of his specialties: Prajnaparamita, Vinaya and Abhidharma, logic and debate, and Dzogpa Chenpo. The outstanding disciple of Patrul Rinpoche, named Nyoshul Lungtok Lama, Tenpai Nyima, was the Dzogchen chodak. It is his lineage teachings that became the tradition of Nyingthig practice at Kathok Monastery. It is the Kathok tradition that Nyoshul Khenpo follows. It is said that one hundred thousand Kathok yogis have attained the rainbow-light body of perfect enlightenment through practicing this particular path.

Nyoshul Monastery in Derge, eastern Tibet, was built by Nyoshul Lungtok's Kathok followers. Khenpo Ngawang Palzang, Nyoshul Lungtok's Dharma successor, became the first abbot there. This highly realized *khenpo*, Ngawang Palzang, raised and educated Nyoshul Lungtok's tulku, Shedrup Tenpai Nyima, who later succeeded him as head of Nyoshul Gompa. Although the current Nyoshul Khenpo Jamyang Dorje studied with Khenpo Ngawang Palzang, Shedrup Tenpai Nyima was Nyoshul Khenpo's root guru.

Nyoshul Lungtok, Patrul Rinpoche's disciple, had five outstanding disciples: two were lingpas or treasure masters, and three were accomplished Dzogchen khenpos. Supreme among them was the aforementioned Khenpo Ngawang Palzang, also known as Khenpo Ngakga. He was an emanation of both Longchenpa and Vimalamitra. His collected works are in ten volumes, and his tulku is presently alive in Tibet.

Khenpo Ngakga was the root guru of Jatral Rinpoche Sangye Dorje. Ngakga was an illustrious disciple of Azom Drukpa, one of Jamyang Khyentse Wangpo's realized disciples, as well as the Dharma successor of Nyoshul Lungtok Tenpai Nyima. Khyentse Wangpo himself had received the Longchen Nyingthig transmission from Jigme Gyalwai Nyugu, as well as from disciples of the Dodrup Chen line, so in these outstanding masters both lines merged.

Lerab Lingpa was the first of the five great disciples to come to Nyoshul Lungtok, and he attended him for years. One of the leading Kathok khenpos of the time was so impressed by Lerab Lingpa's great certainty concerning the view, meditation, and action of Dzogpa Chenpo—which he had achieved without exhaustive intellectual studies—that he too became a devoted disciple of Nyoshul Lungtok Lama, after Lerab Lingpa told him that he had attained his realization through the unique Men Ngag Nyengyud Chenmo, the Extraordinary Oral Pith-Instructions of Nyoshul Lungtok and Patrul Rinpoche. When Lerab Lingpa became the Dzogchen teacher of the Thirteenth Dalai Lama, and Jatral Rinpoche taught the Reting Regent who succeeded him, this particular lineage became further renowned.

This lineage of Longchen Nyingthig is as follows:
Vimalamitra and Guru Rinpoche (8th century)
Gyalwa Longchenpa (1307-1363)
Rigdzin Jigme Lingpa (1729-1791)
Jigme Gyalwai Nyugu
Patrul Rinpoche (1808-1887)
Nyoshul Lungtok Tenpai Nyima
Khenpo Ngawang Palzang (1879-1941)
Nyoshul Lungtok Tulku, Shedrup Tenpai Nyima
Nyoshul Khenpo, Jamyang Dorje (1926-)

Nyoshul Lungtok Tenpai Nyima considered the *nyongtri* or experiential instructions teachings of Nyingthig so precious, that he
made erudite lamas of great stature—including Jamyang Loter
Wangpo, Khenpo Tenphel, and other great khenpos—wait a long
time and promise to truly practice, step by step, before he imparted
to them the *Triyig Yeshe Lama* of Jigme Lingpa according to the
nyongtri way, offering personal instructions and guidance based
on the spiritual experience of each individual practitioner. Later,
Loter Wangpo—one of Dilgo Khyentse Rinpoche's main gurus,
who transmitted those teachings to Khyentse Chokyi Lodro and
Dilgo Khyentse—noted in the margins of a *Triyig Yeshe Lama* text
(which Khenpo Rinpoche has seen), his experiences progressing
through *rigpai tsebeb*, the third Togal vision.

JIGME GYALWAI NYUGU

Jigme Gyalwai Nyugu was the illustrious disciple of Rigdzin Jigme
Lingpa. He became the root guru of Dza Patrul Rinpoche. He used
to receive teachings from Jigme Lingpa, go into retreat and practice for months in solitary places, then return to his enlightened
teacher for further instructions.

Once Jigme Gyalwai Nyugu was practicing Dzogchen meditation in a cave in Tsenrong for two or three years. Despite severe
physical hardships, he practiced continuously with joyous diligence. One day, after his afternoon meditation session, he left his
cave and gazed at the sky, which was brilliant blue with one immense white cloud. He had the feeling that his lama, Rigdzin Jigme
Lingpa, and all the gurus of the lineage were in that cloud. Praying to them with fervent devotion, he lost consciousness.

At the moment when he regained his senses, his mind and the guru's mingled, and he recognized the *rigpai nelug*, the natural original state of primordial awareness. This was due to his unhesitating devoted prayer, the blessings of the lineage, and the intensive practice he had been engaged in. Thus he realized the absolute nature of mind and of all things. Those three spiritual factors are needed to gain realization: devotion, blessings, and awareness practice. One will not achieve it by mere study and analysis.

At that very moment Gyalwai Nyugu's mind was mixed with the mind of the guru, the *dharmakaya*, and he realized the *chonyi kyi gong*, the absolute *dharmadhatu* realization or buddha-mind. That was the *nyamshak*, the meditation. As the *je thob* or post-meditation, the power of his wisdom developed immensely, and he spontaneously understood all the teachings of the Buddhadharma without being taught.

When Gyalwai Nyugu reached realization, he decided to descend from the mountain cave where he had been meditating in order to visit his lama. He had been staying there in the most austere fashion, as an unknown yogi with no patron or assistants, with no supplies or contacts, just an ordinary mountain hermit, unknown to anyone. Later, Jigme Lingpa named him Jigme Gyalwai Nyugu, the Fearless Son of the *Jinas* or Conquerors, meaning Buddhas, in recognition of his accomplishment. But at this time, he was completely unknown and alone. He had decided to stay in retreat, meditating on that mountain, until he either reached awakening or died in the attempt. He attained realization, thus fulfilling his vow.

When he decided to descend from the mountain he was in terrible physical condition. Halfway down, he collapsed. He thought, "I'm accomplished, but now I can't benefit beings. I'm just going to die here alone in this wilderness, but that's all right." Then he prayed wholeheartedly to Jigme Lingpa to be able to fulfill the aims and aspirations of others and oneself.

Eventually two fierce savages with feathers in their hair appeared carrying some maize and meat. They gave him food, and after a few days he regained his strength. Then he continued on until reaching some villages where he could find shelter. When he finally reached Jigme Lingpa, the lama told him that it had been the two Dharma protectors of that place, Tsari, who were emanations of Shingkyong and his consort, part of the retinue of the Gonpo Mahakala, who had appeared in the guise of two wild men to protect him and give him food. Rigdzin Jigme Lingpa told Gyalwai Nyugu he had reached the *chonyi zaysar* level of Trekchod (not the same as chonyi zaysar of Togal), the ultimate level of Trekchod, realizing the actual nature of primordial awareness. After that, Jigme Lingpa bestowed upon him the name of Jigme Gyalwai Nyugu, in accordance with the prediction Jigme Lingpa had received that he would have four great disciples named Jigme.

Jigme Gyalwai Nyugu was originally from Kham. He had left his native place years before and spent many years practicing and receiving teachings in the region around Lhasa and Tsari. After Gyalwai Nyugu's great awakening, Jigme Lingpa directed him to go back to Kham and meditate on a mountain called Tramolung, a mountain in the shape of the copper colored mountain of Zangdok Palri, adding that he would benefit multitudes. In accordance with his master's instructions, Gyalwai Nyugu went to Tramolung.

He had left Kham so long ago that no one recognized him or knew of him. He was alone, just carrying his bag on his shoulder, when he arrived at that mountain in the north of Derge. It was totally uninhabited, with neither people nor animals, with sparse vegetation. The nomads took herds there in the summer, but they lived further north, at lower altitudes the rest of the year.

The nomads were leaving when he arrived. He had no supplies or shelter, but he followed his guru's order and stayed in a cave he happened to discover. Living conditions were extremely harsh, but he decided he would rather die there than fail to fulfill his omniscient guru's wishes. And so he subsisted, meditating most of the time and foraging for whatever grass and shrubs might be found palatable.

After several months, a group of travelers on horseback passed by. One of them, a man dressed in white and riding a white horse, called to Gyalwai Nyugu and said, "What are you doing there? You are supposed to follow your guru's prophecy by dwelling up *there!*" And he pointed to a cold, desolate place even higher up the windswept mountainside, where there was no shelter or wildlife.

Gyalwai Nyugu knew it was a guardian admonishing him, and he immediately moved to that spot. There he remained for twenty-one years, while his fame spread and disciples gathered. Later,

Patrul Rinpoche scolded disciples, saying that Jigme Gyalwai Nyugu had stayed for twenty-one years, while they could not even meditate there for a few years.

Khenpo Rinpoche says he himself never visited that holy place, since it was far from where he was, but that Dilgo Khyentse Rinpoche has visited it, and it was totally uninhabited. Khenpo Rinpoche remarks that neither Gyalwai Nyugu, Patrul Rinpoche, nor Nyoshul Lungtok ever built monasteries or accumulated anything, but simply let things come and go in the most carefree way, relying on nothing other than the inmost spirit of Dharma.

In the beginning of Gyalwai Nyugu's stay there, before he became known, he almost died from the severe hardships he endured. When he thought he was about to die, he recalled that once before the protectors had appeared to save him, so again he prayed fervently to his guru Jigme Lingpa.

Suddenly a young girl appeared in that completely barren land, carrying a pot of home-made yogurt. She asked him what he was doing there. He said he was meditating. She said, "How can you meditate, you have no food?"

Gyalwai Nyugu had doubts about this occurrence and did not want to accept the food offering. He thought it might be a trick by demons trying to deceive and obstruct him. Again he prayed intensely to Jigme Lingpa. The sky was completely clear and blue, but in a white cloud Jigme Lingpa suddenly appeared and said, "If the roots of the tantric commitments (*samaya*) of the yogi are not degenerated, the gods and spirits will always provide sustenance." Then he disappeared.

Thus Gyalwai Nyugu's doubts were cleared. He recognized the girl as the protector, Dorje Yudronma. Accepting the curd, he regained his strength and could meditate for many more months.

Eventually, the nomads returned with their herds. One of them saw Jigme Gyalwai Nyugu's head from behind, in that empty, barren landscape. He wondered if it was a man or a demon, and was afraid to approach. The nomad went to the nearest village and related what he had seen. He was asked if the head had remained or disappeared.

When he said it had remained, his friends told him that it must be a man there. The nomad returned, and shouted from a distance, "Who are you? What are you doing?"

Gyalwai Nyugu replied, "Meditating a little." Thus he became known as a solitary yogi living in that remote place.

When the nomads returned from the village they offered food to Gyalwai Nyugu, along with a thick blanket woven of yak's wool, with which he made a crude shelter. He had been living in a depression or hole in the ground, but now he erected a small shelter, with some sticks holding up the blanket. When they asked him why he was there, he said that his lama told him that he should meditate there, and he would thus benefit many beings, so that is what he was doing. Gradually his renown spread, as he remained in prayer and meditation for decades. Hundreds of yogis, in tents and lean-tos, gathered around him on that mountain during his lifetime.

Gyalwai Nyugu became known as a lama with marvelous inner realization and spiritual qualities. Of his thousands of disciples, the main ones were Dza Patrul Rinpoche and Jamyang Khyentse Wangpo, the famed first Khyentse. His lineage—the practicing lineage of the pith-instructions of Dzogpa Chenpo—spread widely. Through those two great disciples and their followers, it is still alive today. In that way he benefitted innumerable beings in this world. It is impossible to assess his inconceivable Buddha activity in other realms of existence.

When those practitioners meditated on Dzogchen, their only aim and interest was to realize the absolute nature of the mind and reach perfect enlightenment. They had no other aims, no other work to do. They did not have many thoughts, ideas, and projects. Jigme Gyalwai Nyugu thought to himself, "I shall realize the nature of the mind. Even if I die, I shall do this and nothing else." He was not like worldly people who have many things to do. For practitioners like Gyalwai Nyugu, it is very simple. They just think, "I shall stay here and practice until realization."

From a worldly point of view, it seems strange and difficult to understand—someone just sitting and meditating alone on a windswept mountain, with no food, just eating grass. It seems very strange. Milarepa, for instance, meditated for eight years in a cave. His body became ravaged, blue-green, and emaciated, though he had come from a good family. Tibetans used to say, "Work well or you will end up like Milarepa." But for Milarepa it was the only thing he found meaningful and was interested in. Once, Milarepa met some attractive young girls on the road who were frightened by his terrible appearance. They made a wish never to be reborn in such a state. Milarepa said, "Even if you want to, you cannot be reborn like this."

So this is the story of Jigme Gyalwai Nyugu and how he attained realization. Of course there are many other stories. Patrul Rinpoche praised his master in the opening verse of his famous collection of his teacher's oral Dzogchen pith-instructions, *Tsiksum Nedek, Three Incisive Pointers*:

> View is like the infinite vast expanse, Longchen Rabjam.
> Meditation is like light-rays of wisdom and love, Khyentse
>   Ozer (Jigme Lingpa).
> Buddha activity is like the bodhisattvas.
> Jigme Gyalwai Nyugu, to you I pray.

PATRUL RINPOCHE

Dza Patrul was the main disciple of Jigme Gyalwai Nyugu. He was the third incarnation of a Chenrezig *siddha* named Palgyi Samten Rinpoche. The second incarnation had died in his twenties. The story is that during an empowerment (*wang*), he had touched with his rosary a girl who was receiving the wang, an act which—for a Tibetan monk—was considered as bad as touching a corpse. His teacher scolded him, saying that everyone saw it happen and now his reputation was ruined. The tulku answered that it was karma and that he could not help but do it.

Soon after the incident he died. The girl later had a baby boy, who was that tulku's incarnation—Dza Patrul Rinpoche. He was compassionate Chenrezig in human form. Moreover, it is said that in a former life he had been the eighth century Indian pandit Shantideva, author of the *Bodhicaryavatara*.

Patrul received his name from the first Dodrup Chen Rinpoche, Jigme Trinley Odzer (Jigme Lingpa's disciple), who recognized him as Palgyi Trulku (abbreviated as *Pal-trul* or Patrul). He studied at Dzogchen Monastery and became very learned.

Patrul Rinpoche's root guru for Dzogpa Chenpo teachings and transmission was Jigme Gyalwai Nyugu. From him he received all the Nyingthig teachings, transmissions, and whispered pith-instructions. He also received innumerable Dzogchen teachings from many lamas, including the first Dodrup Chen Rinpoche, Shenphen

Thaye, and others. He received the experiential guidance or nyongtri of Dzogchen Longchen Nyingthig from Jigme Gyalwai Nyugu. (This is similar to Dilgo Khyentse Rinpoche, who received countless Dzogchen and other teachings from many lamas, and received the main Dzogchen transmission from Shechen Gyaltsab Rinpoche. Khyentse Rinpoche received this particular Longchen Nyingthig nyongtri from Jamyang Khyentse Chokyi Lodro, as did the present, fourth Dodrup Chen.)

After receiving his teacher's personal guidance, Patrul Rinpoche went to the mountains to meditate, then returned now and again for further instructions. Sometimes he would do *rushen* (a unique foundational practice in Dzogchen) for months. Sometimes he would simply watch the nature of the mind. There are many stories about Patrul Rinpoche, who became extremely famous during his own lifetime, yet remained the most humble of masters.

Patrul Rinpoche had several kings as his disciples, although he himself accumulated nothing, always lived in solitary places, and traveled anonymously. Even in places where he was expected to teach, where people would come from all over to hear him, he would often travel to those places on foot, among ordinary people, unnoticed by anyone.

On such an occasion, he met a woman while traveling. She asked him to carry her small son, and after some weeks together she said to him, "You are a nice man. We get along well. I feel good with you. A widow like me needs a husband, shouldn't we be married?" He declined graciously. She did not even know that he was a learned and perfectly accomplished lama. Later, much to her amazement, she found him sitting on the grand lama's teaching throne in a nearby monastery, surrounded by a great multitude.

Patrul Rinpoche once was unceremoniously sent away by the kitchen attendants when he came to meet his colleague, the famous Jamyang Khyentse Wangpo. When Khyentse Wangpo heard what had happened, he sent his attendants to search for Patrul, to no avail. Khyentse Wangpo himself also had such experiences when he had traveled alone on foot to study with the great teachers of his time. Once he slept outside, near the courtyard gate of a monastery he was visiting on pilgrimage. The abbot of that monastery later came to Khyentse Wangpo with tears streaming, begging his forgiveness.

Once Dza Patrul was in Laotang, in a big charnel ground inhabited by many spirits and gods. The spirits tried to trick him. There was incredible thunder and lightning, voices in the air, and magical illusions. Patrul Rinpoche overcame all that by praying to his root guru, and realizing the ultimate nature of things as they are. Through that realization vast knowledge of all the scriptures naturally unfolded in his heart. Although he had studied widely before, his knowledge and understanding became infinitely greater. Prayer and devotion are very important. The *mahasiddha* Do Khyentse Rinpoche Yeshe Dorje told Patrul Rinpoche that just as Shakyamuni Buddha had subdued the four demons in one instant under the bodhi tree, so had he, Patrul.

Patrul Rinpoche's collected works number many volumes, although many of his writings were never included. Occasional poems he spontaneously wrote or sang were often given to friends and followers, then disappeared like leaves in the wind. He is the author of the popular *Kunzang Lamai Shelung*, as well as many other profound writings.

NYOSHUL LUNGTOK TENPAI NYIMA

Nyoshul Lungtok Tenpai Nyima was the foremost disciple of Patrul Rinpoche. For twenty-five years he received nyongtri from his guru, often going to the mountains and forests to meditate after receiving personal instructions. Patrul Rinpoche always dwelt in the wilderness, with only a few close disciples, and Nyoshul Lungtok was with him most of the time.

Once they were meditating together in the mountains. Patrul Rinpoche asked his disciple if he had realized the nature of mind. Nyoshul Lungtok said that he had not perceived it clearly. They continued practicing. One evening they made a fire and cooked some food. Again the master asked the disciple if he had realized the nature of his mind, and again the disciple said no.

Nyoshul Lungtok had been having a recurring dream, in which he had seen a mountainous ball of black thread that Patrul Rinpoche would unravel by pulling on the end, revealing in the middle a golden statue of Dorje Sempa, Vajrasattva. Patrul Rinpoche said, referring to that dream, "Let's do that now."

It was evening. They were practicing *namkhai naljor*, sky-space yoga, lying on their backs, gazing up into the dark, starry firmament. From way down in the valley they could hear the distant dogs barking at Dzogchen Monastery. Patrul Rinpoche asked him, "Do you hear the barking of the dogs?" The disciple said yes. Patrul Rinpoche asked, "Do you see the stars in the sky?" Nyoshul Lungtok said yes, he could.

Nyoshul Lungtok reflected to himself, "Yes, I can hear the dogs; it is ear consciousness. Yes, I can see the stars; it is eye consciousness. It is all awareness!" In that very moment he realized that all is contained *within*, not outside. *Rigpa*, primordial buddha-mind, is within. Everything is the display of rigpa, intrinsic enlightened awareness.

In that instant, the knot of dualistic clinging fell apart, completely destroyed, and he realized the nature of his mind. All doubts were cut from within, and he perceived naked awareness, emptiness as-it-is. This is due to the power of the meditation practice he did— for he had practiced very hard—combined with the blessing of the guru, in whom he had total faith and confidence.

The questions Patrul Rinpoche asked at that time were merely the support for his transmission of spiritual blessings. To ask if the disciple saw and heard was not an intellectual examination, an explanation of Dharma, or anything like that. It was an intimate, inconceivably immediate way to pour blessings from the teacher into the disciple. In this way, Nyoshul Lungtok attained great realization.

Patrul Rinpoche told Nyoshul Lungtok not to teach Dzogchen until he was in his fifties. Then he was to teach it to whomever he wished. Dza Patrul Rinpoche also predicted that Nyoshul Lungtok would later meet an incarnation of Vimalamitra, who would become the holder of the lineage. Nyoshul Lungtok therefore meditated until he was in his fifties, then began teaching.

Patrul Rinpoche said that Vimalamitra would emanate once every hundred years, and that he, Patrul, would not be meeting him, but that Nyoshul Lungtok would. This was in reference to Ngawang Palzang, Khenpo Ngakga. Patrul Rinpoche instructed Nyoshul Lungtok to give the complete nyongtri lineage to him. Eventually Nyoshul Lungtok had five great disciples, two lingpas or tertons, and three great khenpos, among whom Khenpo Ngawang Palzang was supreme.

Thus Patrul Rinpoche transmitted the nyongtri or experience teaching lineage of Dzogchen Nyingthig to Lungtok Tenpai Nyima

Patrul Rinpoche transmitted his particular *shetri* or theoretical-teaching lineage to Orgyen Tenzin Norbu. Actually, Dza Patrul had four great disciples and Dharma heirs (*chodak*), each of whom upheld one of his specialties, as described before. Nyoshul Lungtok held the lineage of Dzogchen Men Ngag Nyongtri, the lineage received by Nyoshul Khenpo. When Patrul Rinpoche made Nyoshul Lungtok his Dzogchen chodak, he presented his disciple with his own copy of Longchenpa's *Dzodun, The Seven Treasures*. This collection, once used by Patrul Rinpoche and Nyoshul Lungtok Lama, remained as an object of reverence at Nyoshul Monastery until recently, where Nyoshul Khenpo Rinpoche himself had a chance to see and venerate it. No one had opened it for decades.

Patrul Rinpoche passed the explanatory teaching lineage (*shetri*) to Orgyen Tenzin Norbu, who was also known as Khenpo Tenga. This teacher then transmitted it to Khenpo Shenga and Khenpo Yonten Gyamtso (known as Yon-ga), two great khenpos of Kathok Monastery, who were disciples of Orgyen Tenzin Norbu and met Patrul Rinpoche himself. Khenpo Yonga is the author of the excellent commentary on Jigme Lingpa's *Yonten Dzod*. Khenpo Shenga also wrote an authoritative commentary on it. In the house of Dilgo Khyentse Rinpoche's family was a statue of the protector Tseringma, which was filled and consecrated by Orgyen Tenzin Norbu. Khenpo Yonga was the younger cousin of Orgyen Tenzin Norbu, and wrote a renowned commentary on Shantideva's *Bodhicaryavatara*. All these learned khenpos were great practitioners as well as scholars and active teachers.

KHENPO NGAWANG PALZANG

Khenchen Ngawang Palzang was the greatest disciple and chodak of Nyoshul Lungtok Tenpai Nyima. Ngawang Palzang was also called Ngala or Ngakga, and he had a childhood nickname, Ngalu. When he was a small boy, he wore skins and yak-skin boots.

One day his mother took him to Nyoshul Lungtok, who was in retreat at the time, to receive blessings. That very day, Nyoshul Lungtok told his servant that if someone came to see him they should be shown in, although it was customary to turn visitors away during that time. When mother and son came to see the lama and receive blessings, Nyoshul Lungtok received them. He named the boy Ngawang Palzang and gave him a cup of consecrated raisins and a red protection cord for long life. He also told the mother to take very good care of the child, protect him from unclean places, and bring him back later for teachings.

When Ngawang Palzang was eight, his mother brought him again to meet Nyoshul Lungtok and receive blessings. When he was ten he became the servant and disciple of that great lama, accompanying him everywhere, following behind him on circumambulations, listening to whatever teachings he gave wherever he went, sitting with him in private, serving him tea and food, and practicing preliminary practices (*ngondro*) and recitations in his spare time.

One day, when he was about thirteen, he was doing *mandala* practice as part of the ngondro. Nyoshul Lungtok gave him a *thangka*—a traditional Tibetan painting—of Longchenpa, and some *rilbu* pills, relics that are in small statues, along with a hair of Jigme Lingpa. He was instructed to pray to Longchenpa with all these supports, he would certainly get great blessings.

One day, during his mandala practice, he had a vision: There was a white mountain in the shape of a conch, on top of which was a flat, beautiful meadow full of flowers. And he had a vision of Gyalwa Longchenpa holding a crystal in the shape of a heart radiating five-colored light. Then Longchenpa gave him the *rigpai tsel wang*, the fourth initiation, the introduction to the absolute nature of the innate wisdom-mind, rigpa.

At that moment he understood the nature of mind; yet he still considered that Longchenpa was different from him, that they were two. He told his lama, Lungtok Tenpai Nyima, about this vision, and told him what inner state of awakened awareness he had discovered. The lama said, "That could either be dharmakaya or *alaya* (*kun shi* in Tibetan, the ground of all consciousness). We can check that subtle distinction later."

Lungtok told Ngawang Palzang to meditate on bodhicitta, which he did for a long time. Subsequently his teacher trained him through all the sections of Dzogchen, from the preliminary practices of ngondro, through Trekchod and Togal.

In that first vision, he recognized the fundamental nature of his mind. Then, while practicing bodhicitta, he experienced the absolute nature of reality. Later he continued through all the practices, step by step, up through Togal. His initial realization was somewhat incomplete. He still had doubts and needed clarification, so he went through all those sections of practice. That is how nyongtri works, the deep meaning is increasingly plumbed and clarified according to the individual experience of each practitioner.

Only in the rarest cases do realization and perfect enlightenment occur simultaneously. Such practitioners, like Garab Dorje, are called *chik charpa* in Tibetan, meaning all-at-once or sudden awakeners. Generally, one has an experience of awakening, spiritual realization, and then develops towards complete Buddhahood.

SHEDRUP TENPAI NYIMA

The main disciple of Khenpo Ngawang Palzang was Nyoshul Khenpo Rinpoche's root guru, Shedrup Tenpai Nyima. He was the tulku of Nyoshul Lungtok, and took birth as the son of Terton Yeshe Tenzin, one of Nyoshul Lungtok's disciples. Once Nyoshul Lungtok had given Yeshe Tenzin a prophecy, saying that everything was always changing and that one day he, Nyoshul Lungtok, would get blessings from him, his disciple.

At the time, Yeshe Tenzin had not realized what his teacher meant. But when he had a son, some time after his teacher's passing away, and also experienced a lucid dream about Nyoshul Lungtok, he remembered his guru's prophecy and concluded that his son might be his emanation. Therefore, he brought the child to Khenpo Ngawang Palzang and related to him the prophecy as well as his dream. Khenpo Ngakga confirmed it, saying that previously he had a dream of four-armed Chenrezig, and that Nyoshul Lungtok was an emanation of Chenrezig. Thus the tulku was recognized.

Shedrup Tenpai Nyima grew up with his father and received teachings from him. When he was nine, his venerable father, Terton Yeshe Tenzin, passed away. On the third day following the death the boy had a vision that his father, dressed in white, like a yogi, with his hair tied up, introduced him to the nature of his mind. At that moment he awoke, recognizing the true nature of the mind.

Later, Shedrup Tenpai Nyima studied with Khenpo Ngawang Palzang, and received all the teachings, from ngondro through Trekchod and Togal, according to the nyongtri tradition, and developed all the spiritual experiences, visions, and so on. When he clearly realized the nature of the mind, Shedrup Tenpai Nyima told Khenpo Ngawang Palzang about the experience he had had shortly after his father's passing, and discussed the state of mind he had experienced. Khenpo Ngawang Palzang said that this had indeed been the authentic absolute nature, but that he still had to go through all the practices to stabilize his realization and make it unshakable.

Shedrup Tenpai Nyima saw his guru, Khenchen Ngawang Palzang, and Kunkhyen Longchenpa, as completely inseparable: three times he experienced visions of their inseparability. He also had visions of Jigme Gyalwai Nyugu, Patrul Rinpoche, Terdak Lingpa, and others. These events are not recounted in his spiritual biography or namthar, but were told by him to Nyoshul Khenpo Rinpoche personally.

This nyongtri lineage descending directly from Rigdzin Jigme Lingpa is shown in the chart opposite.

NYOSHUL KHENPO

Shedrup Tenpai Nyima transmitted this lineage to Nyoshul Khenpo Jamyang Dorje. Nyoshul Khenpo was born in Derge, east Tibet. He tended animals as a youngster, entered a Sakyapa monastery at an early age (his mother's family was Sakyapa), and later became a disciple of Shedrup Tenpai Nyima at Nyoshul Monastery (part of the Kathok Monastery system), a *gompa* in Derge with a few hundred monks and a monastic college.

He served as his guru's personal attendant (*shabshu*) for three years when still a boy, undergoing many hardships. A poor novice, he repeatedly had to drive off packs of large Tibetan mastiffs on his alms-collecting rounds. He still has scars on his legs to prove it. He was so poor that he lacked even a grain of rice to offer during all of his mandala offerings, while doing ngondro at the age of twelve. Ultimately, through sheer determination, he excelled in his studies and became exceedingly erudite, completing the khenpo training at the monastic college at Nyoshul Monastery under the guidance of Shedrup Tenpai Nyima, while also undergoing extensive Dzogchen training and numerous retreats, including one year

Dzogchen Lineage Chart
of Nyoshul Khenpo Rinpoche

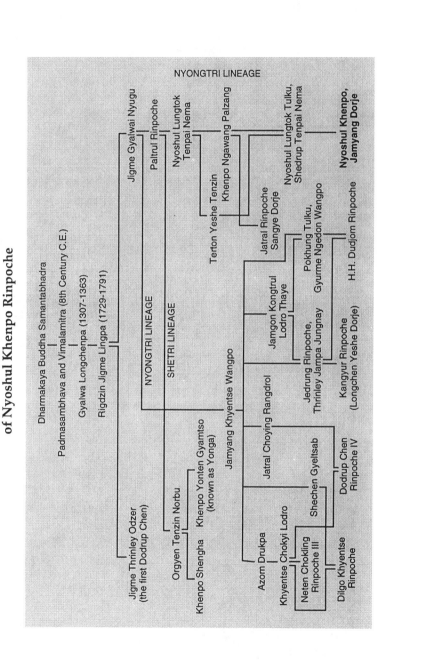

NYONGTRI LINEAGE

Dharmakaya Buddha Samantabhadra

Padmasambhava and Vimalamitra (8th Century C.E.)

Gyalwa Longchenpa (1307-1363)

Rigdzin Jigme Lingpa (1729-1791)

Jigme Thrinley Odzer
(the first Dodrup Chen)

Jigme Gyalwai Nyugu

Paltrul Rinpoche

Nyoshul Lungtok
Tenpai Nema

NYONGTRI LINEAGE

SHETRI LINEAGE

Orgyen Tenzin Norbu

Khenpo Yonten Gyamtso
(known as Yonga)

Khenpo Shengha

Jamyang Khyentse Wangpo

Terton Yeshe Tenzin
Khenpo Ngawang Palzang

Nyoshul Lungtok Tulku,
Shedrup Tenpai Nema

Jatral Rinpoche
Sangye Dorje

Jatral Choying Rangdrol

Jamgon Kongtrul
Lodro Thaye

Pokhung Tulku,
Gyurme Ngedon Wangpo

**Nyoshul Khenpo,
Jamyang Dorje**

Azom Drukpa

Khyentse Chokyi Lodro

Shechen Gyeltsab

Jedrung Rinpoche,
Thrinley Jampa Jungnay

Kangyur Rinpoche
(Longchen Yeshe Dorje)

H.H. Dudjom Rinpoche

Neten Chokling
Rinpoche III

Dodrup Chen
Rinpoche IV

Dilgo Khyentse
Rinpoche

alone, practicing *tsalung yoga* in a cave. Khen Rinpoche is one of the few Dzogchen khenpos remaining today.

He is a long-time disciple of H.H. Dudjom Rinpoche, Dilgo Khyentse Rinpoche, and Kangyur Rinpoche (Longchen Yeshe Dorje), and a close vajra brother of Jatral Rinpoche Sangye Dorje. He is also a Rimé or nonsectarian teacher. Nyoshul Khenpo had twenty-five spiritual masters. He received the Vinaya vows from the Nyingma abbot Thubten Gomchok Lekden, who had received them from the great khenpo of Nyoshul, Ngawang Palzang. Khenpo Rinpoche has written a book chronicling the lives of the main lineage holders in this line, from Lord Buddha and his disciples until today.

Khenpo Rinpoche told a story about his Mahamudra guru, Rigdzin Jampel Dorje, who did a seven-year Tara retreat, during which he completed one hundred thousand recitations of the *Twenty-one Praises of Tara* for each *shloka* of that long and beautiful hymn—twenty-one hundred thousand recitations in all. That great lama saw all of Tara's buddha-fields and mandalas displayed. When he passed away he gave one great exhalation, saying he was going to Tara's buddha-field, then he was gone, sitting upright in *thugdam*, clear light meditation, for one week after his last breath.

Another one of Khenpo's Mahamudra teachers, Lama Tashi Tsering, was originally in a Sakya monastery. Later he left everything behind to live like Gyalwai Nyugu. He practiced Dzogchen Nyingthig on a remote mountain in eastern Derge and became a great master of the four visions of Togal. When his body was cremated many bone relics remained in the ashes in the forms of Dorje Sempa, Hevajra, Tara, and other deities, as well as being inscribed with mantric seed syllables.

Khenpo Rinpoche's Sakyapa teacher was Khenchen Kunga Gyaltsen. Khenpo received the Lam Dray or Path and Fruit teachings and related transmissions from that lama, who was also a Dzogchenpa. The story goes that Kunga Gyaltsen received the *rigpai tsel* empowerment from a crazy character who spent all his days carrying building stones from a distant river to a wall around a prayer-wheel house, and everyone considered him mad. Later it became apparent that *rushen* was his main practice, and he'd been doing it constantly for twenty years. This explained his uninhibited, unconventional behavior.

Kunga Gyaltsen saw this seeming lunatic and instinctively felt that he was someone special, so he asked that crazy yogi to check his meditation. When the lama Kunga Gyaltsen sat in meditation, the mad yogi hit him on the back with one of the building stones, directly introducing him to the nature of intrinsic awareness. Then the eccentric *rushenpa* ran away. Kunga Gyaltsen, a great khenpo with many teachers and many disciples, regarded him as one of his principle root lamas due to this single encounter, a great awakening, after which he never saw him again.

Several of Khenpo Rinpoche's root lamas are still alive in Tibet. One of them is a great khenpo from Golok named Khenpo Munsel, who is now almost one hundred years old. He spent twenty years in a Chinese prison, where he secretly taught Dzogchen to hundreds of inmates who practiced and accomplished it without the support of studies or outer rituals, during a period when the penalty for religious observance was death. In that prison, Khenpo Munsel taught Longchenpa's *Choying Dzo* and Jigme Lingpa's *Yeshe Lama* from memory.

Nyoshul Khenpo is renowned for his mastery of Longchenpa's writings and for his teachings regarding them. On many occasions he has been requested to take a position as khenpo at the monasteries and colleges of H.H. Gyalwa Karmapa, H.H. Dudjom Rinpoche, Situ Rinpoche, Palyul Rinpoche, Pema Norbu and others. He is the author of *The History of the Dzogchen Nyingthig: the Life Stories of the Vidyadhara Lineage*, as well as other works and songs. He has many disciples in Bhutan, Nepal, India, and Europe.

CONTEMPORARY DZOGCHEN LINEAGES

Both Khenpo Ngawang Palzang and Shedrup Tenpai Nyima understood the nature of their mind during their practice of ngondro, but still they went through all the practices up through Trekchod and Togal. In this particular lineage several of these masters obtained realization suddenly, at once. This type of person is called *chik charpa*.

Jigme Gyalwai Nyugu also transmitted this nyongtri to Jamyang Khyentse Wangpo, the first Khyentse, who realized the intrinsic nature while practicing ngondro. It is said that his great disciple Azom Drukpa did likewise, as did Azom Drukpa's disciple Jatral

Choying Rangdrol, who gave this lineage to the present Dodrup Rinpoche, the fourth Dodrup Chen. H.H. Dudjom Rinpoche received the Dzogchen nyongtri lineage from Phokang Tulku Gyurmed Ngedon Wangpo, his guru, who had been the foremost disciple of Dudjom Lingpa, His Holiness' previous incarnation. Phokang Tulku received it from Jamyang Khyentse Wangpo; he also knew Patrul Rinpoche and Jamgon Kongtrul Lodro Thaye.

H.H. Dilgo Khyentse received this nyongtri lineage from Shechen Gyaltsab, his root guru. The latter had many disciples. Khyentse Rinpoche met him when he—Khyentse Rinpoche—was very young. Shechen Gyaltsab had received this particular lineage from Jamyang Khyentse Wangpo. In this lineage many were like chik charpas. In Jamyang Khyentse Wangpo's namthar it says that he attained realization while doing ngondro.

Kangyur Rinpoche's root guru, Jedrung Rinpoche, Thrinley Jampa Jungnay, received the *sem tri* or nature-of-mind teachings of Dzogchen from both Jamyang Khyentse Wangpo and Jamgon Kongtrul Lodro Thaye. Jedrung Rinpoche was the head lama of Riwoche, a Rimé monastery in Kham where both Kagyu and Nyingma traditions were practiced. He was mainly Taklung Kagyu himself, though he was a great terton and Dzogchen practitioner. Jedrung Rinpoche gave the complete transmission to Kangyur Rinpoche, Tulku Pema Wangyal's late father.

Jatral Rinpoche Sangye Dorje is a direct disciple of Khenpo Ngawang Palzang and guru-brother of Shedrup Tenpai Nyima, Khenpo Rinpoche's guru. Khen Rinpoche also met Khenpo Ngawang Palzang when he was very young, though he studied primarily with Shedrup Tenpai Nyima.

The late Neten Chokling Rinpoche, Orgyen Tobgyal Rinpoche's venerable father, third incarnation of Chokgyur Dechen Lingpa, was a disciple of Jamyang Khyentse Chokyi Lodro, the second Khyentse, who was mainly a disciple of Azom Drukpa. Thus the intact lineage came down to him, like one candle being lit from another.

These are the Dzogchen lineages we have here today, mainly the kahma or oral transmission lineage.

TERMAS

We have described the kahma lineage. There are also terma lineages. Here we will just briefly introduce termas.

Termas are rediscovered Dharma treasures. There are many stories about Kangyur Rinpoche receiving transmission directly from Guru Rinpoche, whereupon their minds were mixed. There are also accounts of his visions of Vimalamitra, Longchenpa, Jigme Lingpa, and others. Dudjom Rinpoche received numerous direct transmissions in the same way. The terma lineages are infinite, direct transmissions from Guru Rinpoche to the treasure master (*terton*).

Thus, between Guru Rinpoche and oneself, in this terma lineage, there is only one person, the great terton who is our teacher. This accounts for the tremendous power and efficacy of such transmissions, even today. The terma teachings of the short and direct lineage are like the warm, fresh breath of the dakinis, from which the moisture of blessings have not yet evaporated. There are, generally speaking, three terma lineages. By adding these three to the three kahma lineages, all the six lineages of Dzogpa Chenpo are included. All kahma and terma are included in those six. (All this is lucidly explained in Khenpo Yonga's commentary to the tenth chapter of Jigme Lingpa's *Yonten Dzo*.)

Termas are generally of two kinds, *gong ter* or mind treasures, and *dze ter* or material treasures. *Gong ter* are extracted from the inconceivable expanse of enlightened awareness, wisdom-mind, by the terton for whom they are intended. They are then taught and written down in a way intelligible to those connected to such a teacher and teachings. *Dze ter* are discovered as objects, such as yellow parchments or scrolls inscribed with dakini-script, ritual objects, reliquaries, jewels, and so on. They may take any form in order to benefit beings.

In all cases, all the various kinds of terma were hidden by Guru Rinpoche—or intimate associates such as Yeshe Tsogyal, Vimalamitra, or Vairotsana—so that the reincarnations of his disciples would later continue to discover them for the benefit of the generations of the future. Tulku Thondup has written an excellent book on this subject, *Hidden Teachings of Tibet*.

As Guru Rinpoche himself said, "Except for a dog's corpse, anything can be taken out as *ter*." This means that terma treasures are inexhaustible mines of teaching, which can appear in any form whatsoever in order to suit the needs of beings. The subject of the termas is truly vast, profound and inconceivable.

Sometimes the terma treasures are delivered to tertons by Dharma protectors, or revealed in dreams and visions. Sometimes the tertons must search for the termas they are karmically destined to find. Sometimes lists of termas and maps are discovered or delivered to tertons, concerning the teachings intended for them to reveal. Sometimes termas are read like books by their discoverers. Often they must be deciphered from the *dayig* or secret symbolic dakini-script in which they appear, or from a single mystic cipher or seed syllable. Sometimes only the terton himself can read, or even see, the terma. At other times everyone can. Occasionally, great efforts are required before the treasure is discovered. One terton wore out several chisels while attempting to extract a terma from a rocky ledge, high up on a precipitous cliff. Others had to offer great numbers of vajra feast offerings (*tsok*), or search for and find the proper consort, before fulfilling all the auspicious circumstances needed to discover Dharma treasures.

In the seventeenth century Terdak Lingpa tried to collect and compile all the termas extant at that time. Yet, until the time of Jamyang Khyentse Wangpo and Jamgon Kongtrul Lodro in the nineteenth century, no complete compilation had been made. For that reason, these two great Rimé masters, tertons themselves, put together the great treasury of terma known as the *Rinchen Terdzo*, including all of the essential root termas of most of the tertons. Thus they prevented many Dharma treasures from being lost. There are now over sixty-three volumes, including seventeen thousand empowerments.

Each terma is considered to be a complete cycle in itself, including all the essential teaching necessary to reach enlightenment. Each terma contains sections which include preliminary practices, the three roots, Dzogchen, and so on, although all the various sections are not always revealed, taught, or written down by the discoverer himself. Depending on various factors, including time and circumstances, and whether such teachings are requested or not by disciples, some termas may be completed later by following incarnations.

A supreme, kingly terton like Jamyang Khyentse Wangpo (1820-1892) unfolded the most comprehensive form of rediscovered Dharma treasures, the renowned *Seven Transmissions* or *Kabab Dun*. His contemporary, Chokgyur Dechen Lingpa (the first Choling Rinpoche), also had the *Kabab Dun*, in a far less extensive form. The first Khyentse's revelations and writings, as well as his life, are completely astounding.

The Nyingma kahma—including all the *sadhanas* practiced at the time of Guru Rinpoche and transmitted from guru to disciple through the long unbroken lineage—was first gathered together, edited, and published in the seventeenth century by the two great brothers of Mindroling, Terdak Lingpa Gyurme Dorje and Lochen Dharma Shri. One was a very great terton, and the other a great translator. To the oral traditions they added their own termas and commentaries, making forty-two volumes in all. H.H. Dudjom Rinpoche did the same. For an introduction to Dudjom Rinpoche's dozens of volumes of writings, see *The Nyingma Tradition of Tibetan Buddhism.*

Other outstanding tertons include Guru Chowang, Rigdzen Godem, Pema Lingpa, Ratna Lingpa, Sangyay Lingpa, Dorje Lingpa, Nyangral Nyima Ozer, Jatshon Nyingpo, Terdak Lingpa, and Longsel Nyingpo. There are said to be five great kingly tertons, one hundred major tertons, and one thousand minor tertons, though one should understand that the actual number of tertons is countless, and the number of termas, like the tantras, is inconceivable. One can read about many of the tertons in Jamgon Kongtrul Lodro Thaye's *Lives of the One Hundred and Eight Tertons* in the *Rinchen Terdzo*, which is as yet untranslated.

His Holiness Dudjom Rinpoche's previous incarnation, Trakthung Dudjom Lingpa, was a great terton of the last century who displayed remarkable powers as well as a very wrathful temperament. A great Phurba (Vajra Kilaya) siddha, he was said to be nearly illiterate, employing thirteen full-time scribes to commit his revelations to writing. He was like the crazy-wise siddhas of old.

THE PROPHECY

Once, Khenpo Ngawang Palzang, disciple of Nyoshul Lungtok Tenpai Nyima, had a dream in which he saw a big *stupa* in India. It was the largest one erected by King Ashoka, filled with Buddha's relics. It was being destroyed from top to bottom. A big river was coming to wash everything to the ocean in the western direction, where the entire ocean became red as this stupa fell into it, as if crumbling from a big rock into the water. At that moment, a voice from the sky said that millions of beings living in the ocean would be benefitted by this stupa.

Ngawang Palzang reported this dream to his lama, Nyoshul Lungtok, who said nothing. Later, Nyoshul Lungtok said in this regard, that the teachings of the Buddha, then being practiced in the East, would be destroyed there, but that they would go to the West and benefit many beings. The voice in the dream had said that beings will be benefitted and will "see the truth." That is explained as meaning they will see or understand absolute truth. It doesn't necessarily mean they will all realize absolute truth, but they will be benefitted greatly by receiving the teachings and understanding their truth.

Nyoshul Khenpo Rinpoche commented that this stupa represented the basis of the teachings of Buddhism, which are being destroyed in the East but will spread more and more in the West. When the voice in the sky said that beings will be benefitted greatly and see the truth, it means one million beings will realize absolute truth, and that beings all over the West will be greatly benefitted by these teachings, which will spread widely.

This is an important and significant prophecy, particularly in connection with Nyoshul Khenpo's own particular Dzogchen lineage and teachings. It comes from two of the main figures in this Nyingthig lineage, Patrul Rinpoche's eminent Dharma heir, Nyoshul Lungtok, and the latter's foremost disciple, Khenpo Ngawang Palzang. If one really meditates on the true meaning of Dzogpa Chenpo, one will undoubtedly have true realization.

DZOGPA CHENPO PRACTICE

For ordinary individuals, Buddhahood seems very far away indeed. However, for Dzogchen practitioners it is not so very difficult. All other paths, both within and outside of Buddhism, are like the preliminaries for Dzogpa Chenpo, the Peak Vehicle. Dzogpa Chenpo includes all the other ways and teachings, and is complete in itself. All other Dharmas find completion in it and lead to it, like rivers emptying into the great sea. Other Dharmas have conflicting viewpoints, Dzogchen resolves them all.

Dzogpa Chenpo is the extremely short, swift, direct path to total enlightenment in this lifetime. It is without great hardships. Other paths are like roads leading to a distant house; Dzogchen is like being in that house. This *amrita*-like Dzogchen Men Ngag Nyengyud of the vidyadhara or rigpa-holding lineage is the most precious and refined essential quintessence of all possible teachings. It allows us to perceive the most subtle levels of how things are and how everything actually manifests, and makes it possible for us to swiftly become totally realized, fully awakened, free. If we practice it now, there will certainly be immense benefits for Westerners everywhere in the future.

There are infinite subtle and profound detailed explanations about all the Buddhist teachings, and about Dzogchen too, but it all depends on meditation practice. That is the most essential thing. One must experience the teachings for oneself, and present one's own experience, understanding, or realization to a realized master, one's own kind teacher, in order to receive the master's assessment and advice. The teacher cannot simply present realization to you. But an authentic, qualified Dzogchen master can easily guide a suitable disciple in the nyongtri manner to the attainment of supreme accomplishment without many hardships, or detailed teachings and intellectual explanations and study. All the teachings will be included in those indispensable personal pith-instructions. Therefore, one should rely totally on that.

Gyalwa Longchenpa says about Dzogpa Chenpo: "It is in perfect accord with all teachings, and is supreme."

It is the purpose of this Dzogchen practice to clearly establish a view that leads directly to realizing that the very nature of one's own mind is the absolute nature. We must not be satisfied with mere intellectual understanding or knowledge about it. That will not free or liberate us. We must develop great, unshakable, inner certainty concerning that fundamental intrinsic nature. All the various practices are the means for developing, progressing, and stabilizing that certainty. This simple yet profound practice, connected with Trekchod or Cutting Through meditation, is explained in Patrul Rinpoche's *Tsiksum Nedek, Three Vital Points Which Strike the Essence.*

Even if Gyalwa Longchenpa, or the primordial Buddha Kuntuzangpo, were to appear suddenly before us in a marvelous vision of rainbow light, that would be nothing compared to having before us Tulku Urgyen Rinpoche and Chatral Rinpoche, living Buddhas, like Padmasambhava himself, who can speak Dzogpa Chenpo directly into our ears. These great teachers are the peerless living lineage holders embodying all the deities, teachers, and teachings.

LINEAGES AND TEACHERS

Sometimes a lama can have many teachers and receive countless transmissions without any conflict. It is not necessary to have only one root lama. One can perceive all teachers as manifestations or emanations of one's own principle root lama, who is actually like Vajradhara incarnate. In some other cases a single teacher will suffice. A guru is like a mirror; one needs to see one's *own* face, one's true nature. All mirrors reflect only what appears in front of them.

Therefore, it is virtually impossible to completely describe and accurately enumerate all the individual lineages. Many lamas hold many lineages, major and minor. The first Khyentse, for example, who traveled all over Tibet anonymously on foot for thirteen years to gather together all the teachings, had one hundred and twenty-five root lamas. Thus he was able to preserve and transmit all the lineages in a totally nonsectarian manner, sparking—along with Jamgon Kongtrul and Chogyur Lingpa—the Rimé renaissance in east Tibet during the last century. Without mixing things up, Jamyang Khyentse taught each of the many traditions according to its own particular tradition. Having practiced and realized everything he received, he could unerringly teach and transmit all the myriad Buddhadharmas, according to the aspirations and capacities of different disciples.

Our teacher, the late His Holiness Dilgo Khyentse Rinpoche, who died in 1991 in Bhutan, received his main Dzogchen teachings and transmission from Shechen Gyaltsab, a magnificent master at Shechen Monastery in Kham. Dilgo Khyentse Rinpoche also received in detail numerous major transmissions from Jamyang Khyentse Chokyi Lodro and Khenpo Pema Losel Tenkyong. Shechen Rabjam Rinpoche reincarnated as his own youthful grandson, Rabjam Tulku. Khyentse Rinpoche was a very great Rimé master. Of course he is also a terton, as well as Jamyang Khyentse Wangpo's incarnation, Manjushri in person. He is the Dzogchen teacher of H.H. the Fourteenth Dalai Lama, as well as the guru of the royal family of Bhutan. May he be reborn in this world soon!

Someone asked Nyoshul Khenpo Rinpoche himself about his own lineage. He claims that he has no special lineage, just the general Dzogchen lineage, the vidyadhara lineage outlined above. Whoever endeavors in Dharma practice will, like the great Khyentses and Kongtruls, likewise attain the great peace of nirvana and become a lineage holder. Khenpo's special lineage is the practicing lineage.

Khenpo Rinpoche says that there are extant biographies of almost all the lineage masters, written either by the masters themselves or close disciples, with the notable exception of three: Orgyan Rabjam Chodrak, Orgyan Rabjam Palgon (Shri Natha, Jigme Lingpa's Nyingthig guru and a disciple of Orgyan Rabjam Chodrak), and Nyoshul Lungtok Tenpai Nyima.

These biographical sources are diverse and scattered. They have never been compiled in a single, comprehensive, written chronicle. From Jigme Lingpa down through today, it is clear, though mostly unrecorded and taught orally. Before Jigme Lingpa's period some of the details are difficult to bring to light. Khenpo's own *History of the Vidyadhara Lineage* is a small effort in that direction, although more research needs to be done. H.H. Dudjom Rinpoche's famous *Chosjung* is mainly a chronicle about the major figures in Nyingma history. (In English it is a massive and authoritative tome entitled, *The Nyimgma School of Tibetan Buddhism*, translated and edited by Gyurme Dorje and Matthew Kapstein.) Terdak Lingpa compiled and wrote down the biographies of the eleven lamas in the lineage from Longchenpa down to him, so we can read something about them in his writings.

Nyoshul Khenpo Rinpoche repeats again and again that the Dharma does not belong to anyone, since whoever practices sincerely and with zeal attains realization and becomes heir to

Shakyamuni's kingdom, ascends Kuntuzangpo's throne. That does not mean one inherits a worldly position or material objects, but that whoever really takes the teachings to heart and practices them as they are meant to be practiced becomes a holder of the lineage, thus benefiting all beings as well as themselves. That is what Khenpo Rinpoche wants to encourage and exhort us to do. The only purpose of all these teachings, explanations, and stories is to facilitate spiritual practice, not merely to feed the intellect.

These profound Longchen Nyingthig teachings are not the teachings of one person. They are all the teachings of Dorje Chang, Vajradhara. Particularly regarding the nyongtri lineage, it is not merely the teachings of Jigme Lingpa, Gyalwa Longchenpa, or Guru Rinpoche: it is the teaching of Dorje Chang, the vajra-shortcut of Dorje Sempa, the wisdom-mind of Kuntuzangpo expressed in the light of each enlightened lineage master's own experience and realization, tailored to suit his disciples and future generations. We should understand that. In the nyongtri tradition, where guidance grows out of the personal interaction between a practitioner and his teacher according to the meditative experience gained along the path, each individual has direct access to the authentic teachings of Dorje Chang. This is its precious, powerful, blessed, immediate quality, which brings extraordinary results. Let us make the best possible use of it, for the benefit of one and all.

Glossary

alaya (Tib. *kun shi*) The ground of all consciousness or *sem* (mind), which is to be distinguished from *rigpa*—pure primordial presence, innate wakefulness.

amrita (Tib. *dudtsi*) Elixir or sublime nectar.

asana A practice posture, of which there are many; the full-lotus sitting position is one such asana.

atman The self, soul, or supposedly permanent self-essence.

bhikshu A fully-ordained Buddhist monk.

bhumis The ten levels a bodhisattva goes through on the way to fully-awakened buddhahood.

bodhicitta The mind of enlightenment. The altruistic motivation to attain enlightenment in order to benefit all sentient beings. Bodhicitta has two aspects: absolute and conventional. Absolute bodhicitta is truth, *shunyata* or emptiness; relative bodhicitta is love and compassion.

buddha-field So-called paradises where some practitioners may be reborn in order to develop more swiftly toward full enlightenment.

chakra Circle, wheel. The energetic centers in the core of the body linked together by the central psychic-energy channel.

Chenrezig (Skt. Avalokiteshvara) The bodhisattva personifying great compassion, or pure love, kindness, and empathy; often used as a meditational deity. *Om Mani Padme Hung* is his/her mantra.

chik charpa Practitioners who attain the realization of enlightenment "all-at-once," simultaneously, or suddenly; to be distinguished from *rim gyipa*, those who attain realization gradually, in stages.

Chöd Cutting ego. A meditative system designed to cut the roots of self-grasping. The lineage traces back to the eleventh century figures, Padampa Sangye and Machig Lapdron, the female lineage holder.

chonyi kyi gong The absolute *dharmadhatu* realization, or buddha-mind.

dakinis Sacred feminine energy personified as female tantrikas; called "sky-goers," they are like white witches, angels, or deities. The dakini principle introduces the infinite movements or dance of emptiness through all forms. "All women are dakinis, all men dakas."

dayig The secret symbolic dakini-script in which *terma* treasures often appear.

Dharma The Buddha's teachings. Truth. The Buddhadharma is equivalent to Buddhism, the teachings of the Buddha.

Dharma heirs (Tib. *chodak*) Successors to a teacher's spiritual lineage and teachings.

dharmakaya The truth body of the Buddha. The absolute aspect of the Buddha, manifest as formless, luminous emptiness.

dohas A spontaneous vajra song, a song of enlightenment, composed by meditation masters in a lineage stemming back to the accomplished siddhas of ancient India.

Drimé Oser An epithet of Longchen Rabjam; lit: "immaculate light rays."

Dzogchen, Dzogpa Chenpo The Great Perfection or Great Completeness. The nondual teachings of Buddhism, often called "the view from above." It is referred to as Ati Yoga in Sanskrit, and also known as the Peak Vehicle or the Great Consummation.

eight auspicious signs Eight traditional symbols of auspiciousness: an umbrella, a pair of golden fish, a treasure vase, a lotus, a white conchshell spiralling to the right, an endless knot, a banner of victory, a wheel of the Dharma.

Emaho An exclamation of wonder and excitement; can be translated as "wonderful" or "amazing."

empowerment (Skt. *abhisheka*; Tib. *wang*; lit: anointment) A tantric transmission rite, empowering a disciple to practice a particular Vajrayana sadhana.

experiential teaching (Tib. *nyongtri*) A teaching tradition where personal guidance is given by the teacher as the student's meditative experience develops; in contrast to the general, theoretical program of teachings found in books and lectures.

Five Ornaments of Asanga The five great texts which the Indian pandit Asanga received in a visionary way from the future Buddha Maitreya. They are: *Madhyanta-vibhaga, Dharma-dharmata-vibhaga, Abhisamaya-alamkara, Mahayana-sutra-alamkara* and *Uttaratantra*.

gompa (lit: solitary place) A monastery or hermitage.

guru yoga The Vajrayana practice utilizing devotion and inspirational blessings to mingle with the guru-principle and realize one's inseparability from buddha-nature.

gyu The mind-stream; our very own "stream of being."

infinite primordial purity (Tib. *kadak*) The Trekchod Dzogchen view that all is naturally perfect and complete from the outset, not requiring improvement or transformation.

kahma Kahma refers to all the teachings and transmissions passed down through the centuries by the long lineage of teachers and disciples (see **ringyu**). It is in contrast to the short and direct lineage of terma (see **nyegyu**), the rediscovered teachings of Guru Rinpoche and other enlightened ones.

kalpa An eon; a vast period during which a world system arises, persists, and decays.

Kangyur The Tibetan Tripitaka. The Buddhist canon comprised of the three collections of Sutra, Abhidharma, and Vinaya, as arranged in Tibet.

karma (lit: action) The law of cause and effect, which explains how our conditioning works.

khenpo (Skt. *acharya*) An abbot, preceptor or professor.

klesha Obscuring emotions. The five fundamental obscurations or five poisons are: attachment, anger, ignorance, pride, and jealousy.

Kuntuzangpo (Skt. Samantabhadra) This is the nature or state of primordial buddhahood, which literally means "All-Good," a personification of our original pure nature.

Lam Rim The gradual enlightenment path, vastly expounded by Lama Tsong Khapa and other luminaries.

lingpas Tertons or treasure-masters. (See **terma**)

Lojong The Mahayana mind training. It refers to broadening selfish motivation (the search for personal happiness) into aspiration for universal salvation and alleviation of all suffering.

Mahamudra The Great Symbol. It refers to the absolute reality itself: how things actually are. It is also the name of a lineage and tradition of teachings.

Mahasandhi An alternative term for Dzogpa Chenpo, the Great Perfection or Consummate Vehicle; equivalent to Maha Ati, the Peak Vehicle.

mahasiddha Yogic adepts; enlightened sages.

mantra Sacred words of power or incantation, the chanting of which is often used as a meditation device.

maras The four demonic forces or major obstacles to spiritual practice and enlightenment. They are: the five aggregates, obscuring emotions, death, and pleasure.

namkhai naljor Sky-space yoga; a Dzogchen meditation practice mingling finite mind with infinite, sky-like awareness.

namthar A spiritual biography.

namtok Conceptuality, discursive thinking; it refers to the dualistic mind and its speculations.

ngondro The foundational or preliminary practices. The ngondro practice usually includes hundreds of thousands of bodily prostrations, refuge and bodhicitta vows and aspirations, recitations of Vajrasattva's one hundred syllable purification mantra, mandala offerings and guru yoga practice. It is used as preparatory training for tantric practice.

nirmanakaya (Tib. *tulku*) The incarnate bodies of Buddha in this world, such as Shakyamuni Buddha, the Dalai Lama and other reincarnated lamas.

nirvana (Lit: great peace) Freedom, enlightenment; the so-called "other shore" of liberation from samsara.

nyegyu The short and direct lineage of terma from Padmasambhava and other enlightened ones. These masters transmit teachings directly, through their deathless wisdom-bodies, in visionary experience, to the *terton* or treasure-masters who discover and reveal these teachings. (See **terma, kahma, ringyu**)

Nyingthig, Longchen Nyingthig The heart essence of omniscient Longchenpa and Jigme Lingpa, the quintessence of the innate Great Perfection, Dzogpa Chenpo. This is a lineage transmission only imparted to one disciple at a time, rarely to a group. It is considered extremely rare and precious.

nyur de dzogpa chenpo The swift and comfy innate Great Perfection: a path that does not require austerities or arduous practices.

panditas, pandits Learned scholars, authors, teachers and commentators.

Practice Lineage The way of the yogis rather than the way of theory, learning, and scholarship. Milarepa's lineage.

prajna Gnosis, transcendental wisdom.

Prajnaparamita The scriptures of the "perfection of wisdom," the fundamental texts of the Mahayana.

pratimoksha vows Vows of personal liberation. These are various sets of vows taken by monks, nuns, or laypeople, utilized to achieve individual liberation.

preliminary practices See **ngondro**.

pundarika flower A lotus flower; the white lotus.

pure land See **buddha-field**.

rangjung yeshe The spontaneous, self-born awareness-wisdom or innate wakefulness within our nature.

rigpa Innate wisdom or wakefulness; pure presence; primordial being.

rigpai tsel wang The fourth initiation, the introduction to the absolute nature of the innate wisdom-mind, rigpa.

rigpai nelug The natural, original state of primordial awareness; the authentic mode of being.

rilbu pills Small round relics that are placed in small statues, often black or red in color.

Rimé The nonsectarian practice lineage; a movement of the nineteenth century, championed by Jamgon Kongtrul and Jamyang Khyentse Wangpo, to preserve and revitalize the teachings of the various schools of Tibetan Buddhism.

ringyu The long lineage of Dzogchen. It descends from the primordial Buddha Kuntuzangpo, to Dorje Sempa, Garab Dorje, Jampel Shenyen, Shri Simha, Jnanasutra, Vimalamitra, and Padmasambhava, and includes numerous enlightened lamas who followed in their footsteps. (See **kahma, nyegyu**)

rupakaya The form body of a Buddha. Truth or reality manifest in form, rather than simply as formless, luminous emptiness or *dharmakaya*.

rushen Separating or distinguishing samsara from nirvana—dualistic mind from nondual wisdom-awareness, bondage from freedom. A practice unique to the Dzogchen preliminaries.

sadhanas Formal tantric texts and guided meditations in Vajrayana practice.

sadhu Indian holy men, generally of the Vedic or Hindu tradition, they usually wear yellow or ocher robes.

samaya Pledges or commitments taken in association with tantric practice.

sambhogakaya The enjoyment body of a Buddha. The visionary form in which Buddhas manifest for those with purified perceptions.

samsara Bondage, delusion. The cycle of suffering, conditioning, death, and rebirth.

sangha Traditionally, the monastic community. More broadly, it can also include yogis, yoginis, and even the entire community of Buddhist practitioners.

sarva mangalam "May everything be perfectly auspicious." A common benediction at the beginning or end of Sanskrit texts.

sem The finite, dualistic, rational mind. Discursive, conceptual mind.

sem kye A term for bodhicitta in Tibetan—lit: "generating the bodhimind"—the flowering or blossoming of the selfless heart of wisdom and compassion.

sem tri The essential, nature-of-mind teachings of Dzogchen.

shabshu The personal attendant of a lama.

shamatha meditation Concentrative or calm abiding concentration, it leads to single-pointed concentration.

shastras The commentaries on the canonical teachings of the Buddha.

shetri The theoretical or explanatory teaching lineage. (See **nyongtri**)

shlokas Verses of poetry written in meter.

shunyata The teaching of the Mahayana that everything is empty and open by nature, lacking in inherent, separate self-existence.

siddhas Adepts. See **mahasiddhas**.

six perfections or paramitas The six qualities perfected by a bodhisattva on the path to Buddhahood: generosity, ethical discipline, patience, diligence, meditative concentration, and wisdom. They are six principles of enlightened living.

stupa (Tib. *chorten*) Large bell-shaped reliquary monuments in which blessed relics of enlightened Buddhist sages and saints are enshrined.

Tangyur The authoritative collection of commentaries by Indian masters as compiled in Tibet.

tantric commitments See **samaya**.

tathagatagarbha Innate buddha-nature, absolute aspect of bodhicitta; it is rigpa, the heart of Dzogchen experience and realization.

terma Terma refers to the previously hidden, rediscovered teachings of the short and direct lineage (*nyegyu*) from Padmasambhava and other enlightened ones. These masters transmit teachings directly, through their deathless wisdom-bodies, in visionary experience, to the terton (treasure-masters) who discover and reveal these teachings.

thangka A traditional Tibetan scroll painting, hung on the walls of a temple or over an altar, often depicting meditational deities and mandalas.

thugdam Clear light meditation, often sustained after clinical death.

Togal Transcendence. (lit: leaping over) A visionary practice in the Dzogchen tantras, even more secret than Trekchod.

Trekchod Cutting Through, or Seeing Through: the main Dzogchen naked awareness practice. A so-called secret practice in the nondual Dzogchen teaching and practice tradition.

tsalung yoga The inner Vajrayana yoga involving *tsa*—the *nadis* or psychic channels; *lung*—the *prana*, energy or breath; and *tigle*—the sphere of mind or *bindu*.

tsampa Roasted barley flour, Tibet's staple food.

tsawai lama Root guru, one's own main spiritual teacher.

tulku The emanation of a realized being, commonly used to refer to the manifestation of a bodhisattva or the reincarnation of a high lama who has passed away.

tummo Mystic heat yoga. A way of utilizing breath, chakras, inner light, and heat to heat up the bodily crucible and realize enlightenment.

Vajrayana The diamond Vehicle or Tantric Way; the third of the three-vehicle approach of Tibetan Mahayana Buddhism.

vidyadhara Awareness holder or rigpa master.

Vinaya The code of ethical precepts and rules. The *Vinaya Pitaka* is one part of the three original collections of the Buddha's teachings: Sutras, the accounts of the Buddha's words; Abhidharma, systematized Buddhist metaphysics and psychology; and Vinaya, the monastic code of ethical behavior and moral training.

Notes

1. The heart.
2. The speech center.
3. Mysore, India.
4. Shedrub Tenpai Nyima was Nyoshul Khenpo's root guru.
5. The two tertons are H.H. Dudjom Rinpoche and H.H. Khyentse Rinpoche.
6. The three doors are body, speech, and mind.
7. The five perceptions refer to oral pith-instructions of the Dzogchen Men Ngag Nyengyud.
8. The three kinds of faith are longing faith, lucid faith, and total conviction.
9. This refers to actualizing the wisdom of perfect buddhahood, and compassion for all beings.
10. The four demonic forces (*mara*) are comfort, death, obscuring emotions, and the five bodily aggregates.
11. The five poisons are the five obscuring emotions (*kleshas*): attachment, anger, ignorance, pride, and jealousy.
12. The three trainings are moral discipline, meditative concentration, and wisdom: the three divisions of the noble Eightfold Path.
13. Chokyi Wangpo is Patrul Rinpoche, author of *Kunzang Lamai Shelung*.
14. Drimé Oser is Longchen Rabjam.
15. Samantabhadra.
16. The nine actions are the positive, negative, and neutral actions of body, speech, and mind; in other words, all actions.
17. Nonreferential three-fold purity refers to perfect nonduality regarding subject, object, and action.
18. "Other teachers" means teachers other than Lord Buddha.

19. The "four mind changes" are contemplations on 1) the precious opportunity afforded by obtaining a well-endowed human existence; 2) impermanence and our own mortality, as well as the death of all that is born; 3) the ineluctable law of karma—cause and effect; 4) the defects of samsara—conditioned existence.

A Long Life Prayer for Nyoshul Khenpo Rinpoche

by H.H. Dilgo Khyentse Rinpoche

ༀ༅། འཇམ་དཔལ་དབྱངས་སོགས་རྒྱལ་ཀུན་དགྱེས་པའི་ལམ།

ཟབ་རྒྱས་ཆོས་ཀྱི་སྣང་བ་སྤྲོ་མཛད་ཅིང་།

རྡོ་རྗེའི་གསང་གསུམ་འཕོ་མེད་གཉུག་མའི་དབྱིངས།

རབ་འབྱམས་ཚེ་ལྷའི་ངོ་བོར་རྟག་བརྟན་གསོལ།

Om Swasti. Jampal yang sog gyal kun gye pai lam,
Zab gye chö kyi nangwa trodze ching.
Dorje sangsum phome nyugmai ying,
Rabjam tse lhai ngowor tagten söl.

You radiate as manifestations of profound and vast Dharma,
The joyous path of Manjusri and all enlightened ones.
May you abide forever in the state of Amitayus, the lord of
    boundless life,
The unchanging, primordial space of the three secret vajras.